COP TALK

REAL STORIES, REAL COPS

SGT. BOB SHERMAN

Tellwell Talent
www.tellwell.ca

ISBN
978-0-2288-3403-8 (Hardcover)
978-0-2288-3402-1 (Paperback)
978-0-2288-3404-5 (eBook)

Forward

M ost books have a "Forward." I decided that I had better write one to explain a few points. Most cops, whether active or retired, occasionally tell some close (non-police) friends about some of their experiences. The friends usually react with a comment such as "Wow, you should write a book!" The cop replies, "Yeah, I should." However, that is the end of it. Cops have written enough police reports that writing a book is not high on their priority list.

I have a total of thirty-one years of police experience. I worked for two departments in suburban Chicago, a sheriff's office in Oregon, and one of the largest city departments on the west coast. I served as a patrol officer, detective, sergeant, crime scene supervisor, and lieutenant. I have a wealth of experience, and experiences contributed by my law enforcement friends, from which to draw.

Somewhere along my life I picked up what I consider a knack for writing. I have written articles for sports car publications and have written countless police-related reports of various types. When I decided to write this book, I knew I could do it, but would have to use a method different than the "just the facts, ma'am" style of writing police reports. The book has taken about ten years of off and on effort. It was a bit of a transition in my writing style, but I think I have managed to make these stories come alive. You, the reader, will be the ultimate judge.

I would be remiss if I did not thank many people: my bride Marie, many retired and active law enforcement friends, and civilian friends, who took the time to read and critique each chapter. I felt that, with all this expertise, there was no need for an editor. But, as it turned out, there was! Although the content was solid, there were quite a few fine points in need of attention. I must thank my friend and fellow "rabbit rescue" person, Paige Harwood, for lending her expertise. She helped take this book to a professional level.

Each story in this book is based on real crimes and incidents. These are not "thriller" or "shoot 'em up" tales. They are stories of everyday life in the world of career policing. Some are funny, some are exciting, some are sad, but each is real. Other than a couple stories that obviously do not involve a crime, each story has a police report on file with some agency in the United States and is based upon that report. I have changed names and places as I felt necessary. In some stories I have created fictional cities and agencies. For clarity, I have used "a.m." and "p.m.," knowing that some readers are not familiar with military time used by nearly all police agencies. In many chapters, I have added or changed details. This way, I can share the stories with you, keep them interesting, and not risk harming anyone. Some stories are written in the first person, and some in the third person; it just depended on what form I felt would be most effective in that instance. Each chapter is independent. You can finish one, and start the next one at any time, without losing track of a story. Remember, these are all based on real incidents. None are fictional. I could not make these up!

Sergeant Bob Sherman, Retired

Table of Contents

Chapter 1

Homicide in a Quiet Suburb

Olympia Hills was a quiet high-end suburban village located south of the City of Chicago. Doctors, lawyers, business owners, company executives, and their families, made up most of the population. Many of the residents were Jewish. In the 1970's, Olympia Hills was considered a very good address.

Mr. Noah Goldberg, and his twenty-seven-year old son Isaac, shared a modest home in the older part of the Village. Mrs. Goldberg had passed away several years prior. Most of the houses in the neighborhood had been built in the 1920's. They were not opulent, as was the new construction on the west side of the Village. All had been custom-designed and were of brick construction. Each home was in immaculate condition, featuring mature and well-maintained landscaping. It could be said that the overall impression was one of understated wealth.

Noah Goldberg owned and operated an import business in nearby Chicago Highlands. It was but a leisurely ten-minute drive from his home to the office. Chicago Highlands was a good-sized city that featured heavy manufacturing, retail, office, and residential areas. At his office, Mr. Noah Goldberg had a desk sited on an elevated platform, toward the rear of his store. From this lofty perch, he would bark out orders to his employees. He also dealt with any upset customers from this position. Isaac worked at the business as the General Manager. Often, Isaac had to run interference between his somewhat disagreeable father, staff, and customers. All this aside, the business did quite well. Isaac had met a young lady, twenty-five years old, by the name of Jodi Wood, through social activities at the local synagogue. She lived with her family in a neighboring suburb. They were planning to be united in a traditional Jewish Wedding, scheduled for June of the following year.

It was a nice summer evening in the south suburban Chicago area. At the Goldberg home, the screened windows and doors were usually left open on nights like that. Noah and Isaac preferred the fresh air, rather than closing all the windows and turning on the air conditioning. Noah enjoyed gardening, and, with a slight breeze, the fragrance of the flowers would drift into the house. Noah was at home catching up on some reading. Isaac had picked up Jodi and gone to an early movie. Afterwards, they would stop and visit with Noah before Isaac took Jodi home. Noah and his future daughter-in-law got on well. It seemed Noah was just as excited about the upcoming wedding as Jodi.

They had gone to the early show, returning to the Goldberg residence at about 8:30 p.m. There was an unfamiliar car, a Ford Mustang, about ten years old, parked in front of the house. Isaac wondered for a fleeting moment whose car that might be. Hand in hand, Isaac and Jodi walked up to the front screen door. It was unlocked as usual. As they crossed the threshold, they stopped and froze.

On the floor in the living room they saw an unconscious Noah Goldberg. A few feet from him they also saw an unknown man lying on the floor, dressed in camouflage clothing, and wearing a ski mask. He, too, was unconscious. A strange, sickening smell permeated the air. The source seemed to come from a towel near the camouflaged man's right hand. There was also a large black duffel bag on the floor. Isaac and Jodi quickly backed out the front door. Jodi ran to a neighbor's home, borrowing the phone to call the Olympia Hills Police Department.

Isaac, having recently completed CPR training at the Synagogue, re-entered the home and checked his father's vital signs. Finding none, he began CPR. After a short time, he felt dizzy and had to go back outside. As he exited the home, the Olympia Hills Fire Department Rescue Squad and the Olympia Hills police arrived. Paramedics took over and noticed the smell right away. They suspected cyanide and called out a warning to everyone. Officer Len James was the first officer to have arrived on the scene, and immediately handcuffed the unconscious man clad in camouflage clothing, as per

Department procedure. As he was being handcuffed, the man began to regain consciousness. The subject's hands had been placed behind his back as he was handcuffed, as was also correct procedure. Officer James hustled the suspect out to his patrol car and put him in the back seat, making sure the heavily screened window of the cage, separating the front and back seats, was closed. A volunteer fire fighter was appointed to watch the suspect as Officer James went back inside to continue the investigation. Paramedics confirmed their initial impression that Noah Goldberg was in fact dead. Officer James designated the house as a crime scene. He took a cursory look into the duffel bag and found coils of rope and two pair of handcuffs. He was recording the names of all present, when the volunteer fire fighter, who had been watching the suspect, ran up to the front door and yelled, "Officer, come out here quick! Your prisoner has slipped his cuffs to his front and is acting squirrely."

Officer James ran outside and yanked open the back door of the patrol car. He reached in and began to draw the now unconscious prisoner out of the car. He smelled that same sickening odor that still lingered in the house. He nearly lost his footing as he felt dizzy and dropped to the ground. His cover officer, Sergeant Lester Brandt, had arrived and took responsibility for the prisoner as the paramedics shifted their attention to Officer James. Other paramedics had arrived and began checking the vital signs of the suspect. Officer James had recovered somewhat and, after several breaths of fresh air, shined his flashlight into the back seat of the patrol car from a safe distance. He spotted an open vial, which would later be examined at the Illinois State Crime Laboratory in Joliet. It would be determined that it had contained cyanide. Meanwhile, the suspect was pronounced dead by the paramedics. It appeared that the suspect had wanted to commit suicide. He succeeded.

Officer James and Sergeant Brandt requested the dispatcher to contact Detective Sergeant Ian Billings, and have him respond to the scene. Billings lived nearby and was there within twenty minutes. After assessing the facts, Sergeant Billings knew that this was going to be an involved investigation and requested assistance from the Cook County Sheriff's Department Major Crimes Unit. Sergeant Billings was a capable detective, but since homicides were rare in Olympia Hills, he wanted to have the help of the experienced Cook County Sheriff's Department detectives, who had dealt with numerous complex cases.

The number one priority would be to identify the suspect. Then, detectives would determine what the relationship of the suspect was to the victim, if any. This would be a key to establishing the motive for the crime. The possibility that other suspects might be involved had to be considered. Sergeant Billings and the Sheriff's Department detectives attended the autopsy of the suspect on the following Monday morning at the Cook County Morgue. Fingerprints of the dead man were taken. The Ford Mustang, which had been parked in front of the Goldberg home and subsequently impounded as evidence, was registered to a Helmut Krueger, at a Calumet City, Illinois address. This lower-end Chicago suburb was about a twenty-minute drive from Olympia Hills. Krueger had been arrested numerous times for various minor offenses, thus his fingerprints were on file at the Illinois Bureau of Identification. The fingerprints on the file card were compared to the prints of the dead man taken at the autopsy. It took identification officers mere moments to confirm that the deceased suspect was in fact Helmut Krueger.

Sergeant Billings contacted Isaac Goldberg at the family import business on Tuesday, and requested he search his files for a customer named Helmut Krueger. Noah Goldberg had been a very meticulous record keeper and had established a comprehensive file for Krueger. It seemed that Krueger had been importing quite a few items from Europe and England, mostly articles that would be classified as war trophies related to Nazi Germany. According to the notes on file, Krueger had been complaining about the duty and import fees charged by Goldberg. These were standard fees, covering duties and brokerage charges. Krueger thought the fees to be excessive. Notes said that Krueger was becoming more agitated and only a week before threated Noah Goldberg at the business, demanding a refund of over one thousand dollars. Noah's notes said that Krueger had stated if he did not get a refund, Goldberg would "pay dearly." Noah Goldberg had made a notation to no longer deal with Helmut Krueger.

Identification found in the personal effects of Krueger included a card showing his membership in the Steelworkers Union. Sergeant Billings made a phone call to the Union office and learned that Krueger was listed as currently employed at Enterprise Steel, a mill on the far Southeast side of Chicago. It was in the late seventies, and the Chicago steel mills were still very much in operation. Billings and the detective team from the Cook County Sheriff's Department went to the steel mill with the purpose of interviewing Krueger's supervisor and co-workers. A summary of the interviews gave a picture of Krueger as a loner, with no friends that anyone knew about. In the conversations that Krueger had with various co-workers, his speech was often peppered with various racist terms regarding, black, Hispanic, and Jewish people. I need not tell you what those were. Many co-workers avoided him for that reason. In addition, Krueger's supervisor said that Krueger had easy access to Cyanide, a chemical commonly used in the mill.

It seemed that a hatred of Jewish people, and a disagreement over money, provided the motives for this crime. To most of us, that would not be enough to kill someone. However, police work sometimes involves dealing with some very bizarre situations and people. Many killers are mentally disturbed. The argument that occurred between Noah Goldberg and Helmut Krueger could well have been enough to set Krueger off. This murder seemed to be the work of one very disturbed person, but all the investigative leads had not yet been exhausted.

There was a lot more to learn about the suspect. With any serious crime, the detective must keep following the trail. Although Helmut Krueger was dead, Detective

Sergeant Billings obtained a search warrant from Judge McKay, at the Cook County Courthouse, to search the house where Krueger lived for evidence relating to the homicide.

The next morning, Sergeant Billings met with the Cook County Sheriff's Department detectives at the Olympia Hills Police Department. Over coffee and some Danish rolls provided free of charge (as usual) by the Olympia Hills Bakery, they reviewed the search warrant and developed a plan. It was a routine procedure: Execute the warrant, remove anyone present in the house, contain the scene and search for any evidence relating to the homicide, seize and catalog the evidence. Each team of two detectives would search every room, and then turn the room over to another team of detectives who would search the room again. In this way, it was unlikely anything would be overlooked.

Two hours later, two unmarked police cars and an unmarked Cook County Sheriff's Police Crime Scene Processing Unit van pulled up to the house where Krueger had lived. After a knock on the door, detectives used a battering ram (commonly referred to as "the key") to destroy the lock and open the door. They were greeted by a sight that, given the history of Krueger as they knew it, was not entirely unexpected.

The entry way led right into the living room. Above the fireplace was a four-foot by six-foot German Nazi flag. On the adjacent wall was a certificate, attesting to the fact that Helmut Krueger was a member in good standing of the American Nazi Party. For those unfamiliar, this was a part of the "White Power" movement that had a small following at the time in the USA. It was basically a group that embraced the doctrines of Nazi Germany. On another wall, was a photo of a German SS officer in full uniform, identified by a note on the back as "My Dad, 12. SS Panzer Division Sturmbannführer Michael Krueger, killed in action, Normandy, August 8, 1944." On the walls, there were displayed various articles of Nazi memorabilia. These items were photographed. A thorough search indicated that Helmut Krueger lived there by himself. This was confirmed by another detective who had been canvassing the neighborhood. Neighbors knew Krueger by sight, and all stated that he was quite a hermit, never even saying hello or goodbye to anyone, or having any visitors. Oddly, they did not even know his name.

The detectives went to the basement of Krueger's home. So far, there was nothing too surprising. This was obviously the home of a Nazi nut case, who acted out and killed a Jew whom, by his nature, he hated. The basement was full of the usual collection of claptrap. The detectives stood in a circle and talked about a plan for the next day. One detective noticed that a wall bookcase had small wheels along the bottom.

Some hallmarks of great detectives are observation and curiosity. The detective called to the others and said, "Hey, let's try pulling this out, there must be something here." What they saw next amazed even these veteran detectives.

The bookcase covered the doorway to a concrete walled room, about twelve feet square. The room had probably once been used to store coal for a furnace that was no longer there. The walls and floor both appeared to have recently been painted a glossy gray. Additional lighting had been installed, as well as two electrical outlets. The purpose of this room became all too clear as the detectives saw, in the middle of the room, a heavy wooden table, about eight by three feet. Bolted to the table were heavy metal shackles for use in restraining arms and legs. There were also two heavy leather straps that could be used to further restrain a shackled person. It seemed evident that Krueger must have planned to take Noah Goldberg prisoner and transport him to his house. If the crime had gone that way, the detectives could only imagine as to how Noah Goldberg would have spent what surely would have been his final hours.

There was no evidence to show involvement of any other suspects. Detectives had determined the motive for the crime and had developed an understanding of the disturbed mental state of the suspect, by means of interviews and evidence. Reports were completed, and the case was classified as "Cleared." Sergeant Billings met with Isaac Goldberg and his fiancée Jodi Wood to explain completely what the investigation had uncovered. Difficult as it must have been for Isaac and Jodi to hear, they deserved to have that information. This was indeed a most bizarre homicide, in what was normally a very quiet suburb.

Chapter 2

Chasing Motorcycles

P ursuits of motorcycles are generally not a productive endeavor for police officers. The idiots on bikes that run from the police have no regard for their own lives, or for the lives of innocent people. Thus, at least in the City of Portland, Oregon, most motorcycle pursuits are terminated in short order by a sergeant, or by the officers themselves. I was, however, directly involved in three memorable motorcycle pursuits, two as an officer, and another interesting one as a sergeant. All three were "wins" for the good guys. You will read about the one that occurred when I was assigned as sergeant, in a later chapter.

The first motorcycle pursuit in my career occurred during my first "full time" police job in the Village of Broadmoor, Illinois. (Prior to that, I was a part-time police officer in another village.) I was working a Friday night graveyard shift, midnight to 8 a.m. In the Village of Broadmoor, the sidewalks were pretty much rolled up after 10 p.m., even in the summertime. Lacking anything else to do, most of us worked a lot of traffic enforcement, referred to as "self-initiated activity." I had my radar gun in action, monitoring Broadmoor road, just east of US Highway 54. I was clocking traffic that was approaching from the rear. The posted speed limit was 25 mph. I caught a glimpse of a single headlight in my side view mirror as my radar unit gave me a reading of 52 mph. Well, here was a customer!

The single headlight turned out to be that of a motorcycle. As it sped by, I pulled out right on its tail and activated my overhead lights. It sped up. My first pursuit! I knew it would be hard to catch a powerful bike. Still, I tried. This included developing tunnel vision and blowing right through two stop signs, oblivious to any cross-traffic. I was lucky in that, due to the hour of the night, there was not any cross-traffic. Units from two neighboring suburbs had come to assist, and one unit found the motorcycle after it had crashed against a concrete median a little west of the second stop sign that we had both sped through. The driver of the motorcycle was quickly located, hiding in the trees close by. It was obvious that he had been drinking, although he was underage. Off he went in my patrol car, handcuffed, to jail.

The night became more interesting when the arrested subject's brother showed up at the police station. Drunk (also under aged) and belligerent, he demanded the release of his brother. In a few seconds, the fight was on. My sergeant deployed oil-based pepper mace, which put a quick end to the confrontation. It also caused us to have to open all the windows of the small police station, where, located behind the front counter, the dispatcher/call taker had no protection other than ten feet of air. Both brothers spent the night in jail. I do not recall what happened with their cases, but both received a lot of attention from Broadmoor Police for years to come. A word to the wise: Avoid getting on a first name basis with your local police officers as a result of your bad behavior. They will give you more personal service than you ever imagined! Both brothers ended up with a never-ending succession of driver's license suspensions and revocations for quite a few years.

My second motorcycle pursuit was while I was an officer in Portland, Oregon. My assignment was at North Precinct, afternoon shift, and I was patrolling the St. Johns District on a warm summer evening. A pursuit of a motorcycle had started near Lloyd Center, a large shopping mall in the far southeastern part of the precinct, several miles away. The pursuit progressed in a general westerly direction, as various patrol units engaged and disengaged, due to the chase becoming too hazardous.

My assigned district was on the northwestern edge of the precinct. From the driver's path, it seemed that the bike would ultimately head my way. I was near Northwest Germantown Road, which led from the industrial area through Forest Park, out to the west suburbs. I had been sent to that location to provide cover for an Oregon State Police trooper on a traffic stop. As I arrived, I saw a speeding motorcycle heading up Germantown road. I checked to see that the OSP unit was okay, cleared, and began to chase the bike. Another Portland Police car, driven by Officer Fred Winslow, was right behind me.

I knew Germantown Road like the back of my hand. Living in a nearby suburb, it was my route to and from work, and I had driven it hundreds of times. At the top of Germantown Road, there is a four way stop sign, where the road intersects with Northwest Skyline Boulevard. Between the start of road at Northwest Bridge Avenue, to Northwest Skyline, there are three miles of hairpin turns and switchbacks. It is a road that sports-car drivers just love.

I figured it this way. There was a chance the driver of the motorcycle would not know the road that well and could go off on one of the tight corners. If he did so, we might just catch up to him before he got up and going again. I would drive as fast as I safely could in that big Dodge Diplomat police cruiser, and maybe I would be lucky.

About a mile up, I was fast approaching a hairpin right turn when my headlights picked up a sight to behold. The motorcycle driver had indeed gone straight off the road and the bike was down. He was frantically trying to lift it up and get going again. I skidded to a stop right in front of him, blocking his path. My cover, Officer Winslow, was right behind me. Both of us must have thought alike because, as we jumped out of our police cars, we each grabbed our nightsticks. We had to quickly stop this guy from jumping on his bike and going again, so we each went to work on an arm, me on his right, and Fred on his left. He dropped the bike and, after quite a few blows, was handcuffed and taken into custody.

With the driver handcuffed in the back seat of my patrol car, it took me about an hour to write up all the traffic citations and reports. Eluding the police is a criminal offense and required booking into jail. The subject of the pursuit had settled down somewhat, and I offered to take him by the hospital to be checked for injuries as a result of the use of the nightsticks. He declined and said that he knew he would be sore the next day. He said he understood why we did what we did. The young man did not seem to be a bad guy, but just a young person who did something stupid. This pursuit ended well. No wrecks, no injuries, no unwarranted risks, subject apprehended. Even the sergeants were happy!

Chapter 3

Graveyard Shift in a Bedroom Community

My first full-time career police job was in the "bedroom community" of Glencoe, Illinois. Many residents took the commuter train to Chicago in the early morning hours, returning in the evening. Most of the women stayed at home during the day. This was the 1970's. The women had roles much like the "Stepford Wives." We did not have a lot of crime in Glencoe. Sure, we had our burglaries, petty thievery, and juvenile matters. For a young officer, with even a little ambition, the job in Glencoe was often somewhat boring. To keep the shift interesting, one had to self-initiate activity.

This was especially true on graveyard shift, midnight to 8 a.m. We had no bars nor any all-night convenience stores. There was nothing to keep us even remotely occupied. This fact was not lost upon the Chief of Police. We were thus expected to enforce various parking ordinances to show some activity. We also were expected to do security checks on commercial buildings. That was okay; it got us out of the police cars and kept us awake. The other obvious way to keep active was by doing traffic stops.

To initiate a traffic stop, the officer must have "p.c." This is "probable cause," meaning reason to believe that a violation or a crime has occurred. Thus, every vehicle with a taillight, brake light, or headlight out was fair game. So were vehicles with missing license plates, obscured windows, and loud exhaust systems. I think you get the idea. Most of the time, a traffic offense warning was given. Sometimes, the stop would yield a drunk driver, a suspended driver, a person wanted on an arrest warrant, etc. Once in a great while the driver would "fail the attitude test." Starting to argue with the officer with words like "Don't you have anything better to do?" Or, "Didn't you sing with the Village People," would often end up with the officer writing a traffic citation that he or she normally would not have bothered with. Some people never get it.

There were an infinite number of separate shared police radio channels in the Chicago area. Information about major crimes in one place could often not be broadcast by the standard police radio to departments in adjacent areas. As a solution to this problem, all police cars in the entire Chicago Suburban area were equipped with a secondary radio, the "ISPERN" unit. This was an acronym for the Illinois State Police Emergency Radio Network. If a major crime, such as an armed robbery, kidnapping, rape, homicide, etc. occurred, and the officer wanted to alert all police agencies, he or she would give out concise suspect and crime information on the ISPERN system. If you went over a minute, the radio would "beep" at you!

One cold winter night at about 2:30 a.m., I had just finished writing one of our obligatory parking violation tickets to a vehicle parked on a residential side-street. The ISPERN Radio crackled with information about an armed robbery. The robbery had just occurred in Madison, a suburb south of Glencoe. We did not share Madison's air. Information about the armed robbery, and the two suspects, was broadcast on ISPERN: "Armed robbery of the Clark Gas Station in Madison just occurred, $150 cash taken. Suspect number one: White male, twenty years old, tall, blonde hair, slender build, dark overcoat. Suspect number two: White male, eighteen years old, shorter than number one, brown collar length hair, slender, blue jean jacket and pants." No vehicle information was available. I always had a clipboard on the seat next to me, as did most cops. If you wanted to write down some information in a hurry, you did not want to be fumbling around. So, I jotted down these descriptions, just in case.

I put the police car in gear and drove about a block to where the side street met US Highway 54. This was one of two main highways that went through the Village, generally in a north-south direction. Before the interstates, U.S Highway 54 was a main commercial route. Now, it was mostly local traffic, but it still was called US Highway 54. I pulled up to the stop sign and saw a blue Chevy Nova northbound. One of its headlights was burned out. This was fair game for the somewhat bored policeman.

I pulled out behind the Nova and got close enough to call in the license plate number to the dispatcher. I turned on the red and blue overhead lights. The car did not stop right away and kept going. Suddenly a brown paper bag went flying out the front passenger window and landed in a snowbank. From past experiences, I figured this was probably some booze being pitched out by underage drinkers. Boy was I wrong!

The Nova continued a short distance, entering the neighboring suburb of Elmwood, with whom we shared the radio frequency. I updated dispatch with the location. The vehicle stopped. As I got out of the police car, the driver of the Nova exited and started walking toward me. He was, white, about twenty years old, slender, blond hair, dark overcoat. It clicked. This guy exactly matched the description of one of the armed robbers broadcast on ISPERN. I drew my Smith & Wesson .357 caliber Magnum revolver, pointed it directly at the suspect, ordered him to stop, and asked for a cover car. In seconds, there were five; a couple of which had already been headed my way. On graveyard shift cops share a common bond. They always head to a traffic stop made by another cop in the area during the wee hours. You never can tell what might happen on what initially seemed to be a routine stop. We took the driver into custody, handcuffed him, and put him in a police car. We then ordered the passenger out at gunpoint. He matched the description of the second suspect to a "T" and was also handcuffed and put in a different police car. I had hit the jackpot. I knew I had the armed robbers!

The Madison officer who took the armed robbery call sped to the scene of our stop. We backtracked to where the brown paper bag had landed. We found that two handguns had come out of the bag and were lying in the snow. One was a nine-millimeter semi-automatic pistol. The other was a six-shot .38 caliber revolver. Both were loaded. I was lucky. This could have gone in another direction. The weapons were recovered as evidence and later would be transferred to the Illinois State Police Crime Laboratory at Joliet. They would be examined and test-fired, so that at trial, it could be established that the guns were fully functional.

We went back to the Nova and did a thorough search. At first, nothing unusual was found. Often criminals stuff weapons and other objects up under the dashboard, so that was checked as well. There I found a wad of cash. The Madison officer and I both counted the money. It totaled $150, the proceeds of the robbery. This would be entered into evidence and documented in the police report. At trial, a jury would likely agree that innocent people do not generally stuff money up under their dashboards.

The last piece of the on-scene investigation was to have a "show-up" of the suspects. Given the facts so far, we knew these were the bad guys. Still, everything must be done to seal the case. An identification of the suspects must be attempted. Case law had held that, if the suspects were brought back to the scene of the crime, i.e. the gas station, it would be prejudicial. However, the victim could be brought to the scene of the arrest to view the suspects. Another Madison officer thus had picked up the armed robbery victim, the Clark Gas Station attendant, and brought him to the arrest location. Each suspect was taken out of the patrol cars, still handcuffed, and illuminated with police car spotlights. The victim, with no hesitation, identified the two as the armed robbers.

This was a well-documented case, supported by overwhelming physical evidence. Both suspects pled guilty to armed robbery. Without my lucky traffic stop, I doubt that the pair of armed robbers would ever have been caught. Sometimes bored police officers find a little excitement, during graveyard shift, in a bedroom community.

Chapter 4

All it Took was a Simple Phone Call

I had been assigned for about a year as a detective in the Chicago suburb of Broadmoor. The detective sergeant and I alternated shifts between days and afternoons each month. We had some overlap so we could exchange information about our cases.

We had experienced a series of residential burglaries in the west end of the village. No suspects had yet been developed. As a detective, once you receive the case report taken by the uniformed officer, you conduct a follow-up visit to connect with the victim family. You want to cover all the bases as to who knew their schedule, did they cancel papers and services, who did the yard work, etc. Most of the time, the service providers were honest and reliable. Still, as a detective, you need to cover all possibilities. So, in the police reports and follow-up interviews, there is a lot of information, if only you have the time to digest the data and do anything with it.

Upon occasion, you have a slow day. You pick up some case files and think about what you can do. On one such slow day, I picked up a stack of the west end burglary case files. I spread them out on my desk and looked for commonalities. In the west end burglaries, most of the items taken were such that juveniles without a vehicle could carry away. Pillowcases and duffel bags, found in the victim's house during ransacking, were the containers of choice used to carry off the loot. This observation started me thinking and analyzing.

As I reviewed the report of the burglary at Mr. and Mrs. Alonzo's home, I noted that mention had been made regarding a teenager who had done some yard work for the Alonzo family. He had knowledge regarding the dates that they would be away on a vacation. These encompassed the time period when the burglary took place. The teenager, James Denmark, did not have key access to the house. I had an address and phone number for Denmark. He lived just a few blocks away from the burglary. I dialed the number.

A woman answered and I identified myself. I told her I was going over some reports about missing property. This was a low-key way to start the conversation. You get a lot further that way in detective work. I said that I had a list of a few items and wondered if anything like them had showed up in her home. I mentioned that the items included a princess phone, a couple folders of common collector coins, and a pair of binoculars. She replied: "Now that you mention it, yes, I think they are in my son James' room." When she confirmed that she would be home for a while, I told her I would be right over.

Ten minutes later, I arrived at the address located in the Village of Hazeldell, a suburb that was right on the north-western boundary of Broadmoor. This area was but a short walk from the west end burglaries. That neighborhood of Hazeldell was composed primarily of apartment buildings and duplexes, generally well kept. I knocked on the door, and Mrs. Denmark answered. We pleasantly greeted one another. Of course, I showed her my identification, and offered a business card. A quick glance around told me that this was a well-kept home. Mrs. Denmark was in the position of many divorced mothers. She was working full-time and doing her best to raise a teenage son who was prone to numerous distracting influences, many not to his benefit. I had my case folder with me, containing Property Receipts. She retrieved several items from James' bedroom, and I receipted each item, placing them in evidence bags which I had brought along for that purpose. She signed the property evidence receipt and I left her a copy as required by department procedure. I told her we would have to talk with James about the items, and she understood. I did not tell her that he was now a burglary suspect. After all, recovered stolen property was all that I had at the time. I knew that we had found fingerprints at some of the burglaries, including latent prints from the Alonzo home. A car taken from another burglary had been dumped close to the Denmark home. James Denmark's fingerprints would not be on file yet because of his prior juvenile status. He had just turned seventeen and, under Illinois law, was now considered an adult. Thus, he was soon to be fingerprinted.

I contacted my Sergeant and partner, Alec Redding, at his home, and told him what I had. He came into the station and together we reviewed the evidence and the case file. We got into our unmarked detective car and went to the Broadmoor High School office. We had decided to pick up James and bring him in for questioning. Broadmoor High School officials were always great to work with; we got on well. The Dean of Boys, Ted Mosovich, had James Denmark summoned from his class to the office. When James arrived at the Dean's Office, we introduced ourselves and made some friendly small talk to put him at ease. James Denmark willingly came along with us to the police station for an interview, so he legally was not under arrest and did not yet have to be advised of his constitutional right to remain silent. The three of us sat down in the interview room, and I opened the evidence bags full of the items recovered at his home. He paled, and we suggested he tell us about the items. He made a full confession to the Alonzo burglary, and to four other area burglaries. He implicated another teenager, whom we arrested later that day. A comparison of the latent prints recovered from the crime scenes was made to the new booking fingerprint cards, containing the prints taken following the arrest of Denmark and his associate. There was a match to each of the suspects, clearly linking them to the burglaries. Pursuant to a plea bargain, Denmark and his associate each went to prison for five-year terms. James needed to be put away. We had a feeling that, no matter what, he would be a career criminal. The public would be safe for few years anyway. This story really tells what most detective work is about. It is not the exciting Hollywood-scripted life people see on the television shows. It is just a lot of follow-up, phone calls, interviews, etc. Most of it gets you nowhere. Sometimes you get a result. That is what a detective is paid to do.

Chapter 5

Gray Lady Down

Deputy Sheriff Mitch Douglas had been serving in the SCAT Unit, an acronym for the Special Crime Attack Team, for several years. The unit had, among other activities, routine vice missions that were done on a random basis, to keep the crooks a bit off guard. Tonight, SCAT was conducting a prostitution sting operation at an up-scale hotel near the Merchandise Mart, just north of the Denver City Limits, close to the airport.

The Sheriff's Department had been successful in stemming the massage parlor business in the last few years, but only by applying constant pressure. But, like squeezing a water balloon, the contents were just displaced. The "outcall massage" business had developed, and freely used the local newspapers to advertise. Everyone knew that the focus of these advertisements was hardly therapeutic massage. The hotels and bars where missions were conducted were very cooperative. They did not want this sort of activity taking place on their premises. Usually, SCAT would make a few arrests at a specific location before the word got out in the sex trade industry that the gals were being taken into custody at that location.

Deputy Mitch Douglas had a damn fine record. He never bragged about it. The results were all statistical. In the last four years, he had more prostitution arrests and convictions than the rest of the five-man unit combined. Mitch was, at the time, a skinny guy with curly red hair, who looked and acted more like he had just come in from the hills of West Virginia, than an undercover cop in Colorado. That is what it took. If one looked and acted like a cop, the prostitutes and the dopers would sniff it out in a heartbeat. To be effective, the police officer had to get them off guard from the very beginning.

So, here was Sheriff's Deputy Mitch Douglas, just lounging around in a very expensive room in a fancy hotel. Big screen T.V., Jacuzzi, and a well-stocked mini bar fridge were standard luxury furnishings. Deputy Douglas had called "Tracie" about an hour before and booked a "massage." She was to come by at 10:00 p.m. It was now 9:45 p.m. The lights were turned down low on the dimmer switch, some cool jazz was on the sound system, and the stage was set for the "lady of the evening" to fall right into the trap. She had probably done this hundreds of times before and would think nothing of the setting.

The Sheriff's Office unit was very close. They took a lot of risks, drank a lot of beer (off-duty), and trusted each other with their lives. The big joke was that Deputy Douglas had his clothes off and on so often that he developed a skin rash. The SCAT team members, assembled in the adjoining room, turned on the state-of-the-art video equipment, which at the time was HBO with a 32" T.V. The "movie of the night" was *"Gray Lady Down,"* with Charlton Heston, David Carradine, and Stacy Keach. They settled in to watch the movie. It was a good way to pass the time until the action started. Please note that this occurred in 1978. At that time, any electronic surveillance equipment was a bit of a challenge to get working correctly. Audio surveillance equipment was the rule for these misdemeanor cases; police video technology was in its infancy. With the arrest/back-up team right next door, a twist of the lock would allow them to quickly be right at Deputy Douglas' side. Wires had been routed through the ceiling panels, and a microphone was taped in place on the back of the headboard. All tests showed that that system was in perfect working order and the equipment functioned as it should. To back up the audio recording, the SCAT team members would also be able to testify that they had heard the conversation between Deputy Douglas and his lady of the evening.

Every jurisdiction has its rules established by the District Attorney's Office. If officers wanted a case issued, they had better play according to the District Attorney's procedures. In these cases, the usual approach by the defense attorney was to assert that the sheriff's deputy had "entrapped" the prostitutes. The DA, in Adams County, went by the interpretation that "entrapment is seducing the innocent mind." When there are two people in a hotel room, exchanging items of value (cash) for sexual acts, nothing "innocent" is going on.

Mitch Douglas was abruptly brought to attention by a soft knocking at the door. His "massage date" had arrived, ten minutes late. He opened the door and saw a very attractive gal, probably in her early thirties. She looked like she stepped right out of a centerfold. She smiled and came right in, excusing herself to use the bathroom. Meanwhile, Deputy Douglas stripped down to his underwear, assuming the character of a typical "John." As she shut the door behind her, he laid down on the bed and spoke quietly toward the microphone, alerting the team to the fact that the "date" had arrived, and that they needed to come through the door when he gave the "bust" signal. Tonight, the "signal" was that he would say something to the effect of "Hey, I'm having a hard time getting into this because you remind me so much of my sister." His "date" emerged from the bathroom, wearing only the flimsiest of lace panties. Without hesitation, she hopped right into bed and pulled down his briefs, grabbing his manhood before he knew it. "Okay, keep cool," the Deputy said to himself. He had to get the statements. "How much is this going to cost me," he asked. One-hundred dollars was the reply. Still amazed at how quickly she acted, he tried to slow her down and said: "You look too much like my sister." Deputy Douglas expected his team to come rushing through the door, but nothing happened. He again said "This is hard, you remind me of my sister. This is not easy." Still, there was no response from the team. Traci laughed and said, "Hey, just close your eyes and I'll give you more than $100 worth of play!"

Mitch told her that he needed to use the bathroom, and he pretended to stumble into the door connecting his room to the one next door, giving it a loud bang. At last, the arrest team came through the door, much to Tracie's surprise. A female deputy was summoned from downstairs to take custody of Tracie.

Deputy Mitch Douglas was not happy. The reader might laugh and think, well gosh, the worst that could have happened was that he would have had a roll in the hay with Tracie. It does not work that way. First, an undercover cop absolutely cannot do that. His credibility would be destroyed. Second, and more important, was that he had a loving and trusting wife at home. She knew about his job and what he was doing. No way would he ever compromise that.

Right after the arrest, Deputy Douglas talked with his team. He needed to find out what the problem was. As it turned out, the team had tuned in to the movie "Gray Lady Down," and had become so engrossed in the film that, not only did they not hear the "bust" signal, but that they had even forgotten to activate the tape recorder. They were not even aware that "Tracie" had arrived. Everyone, except Deputy Douglas, thought that this was very funny. To make matters worse, the police photographer, who entered with the arrest team, had taken a photo of Mitch coming out of the bathroom in his briefs. The photograph was posted in the Sheriff's

Sub-Station office for about a week. Many years later, when the old team got together, this was still one of the team's favorite tales from the "undercover days."

However, let us get back to "Tracie." She appeared on her court date, along with others who were similarly charged. She heard that the Sheriff's Office had the cases on tape. She was never specifically told that there was a tape of her case; she just assumed one existed. She pled guilty.

There is, however, a short "epilogue" to this story. Two more arrests were made that night. The SCAT Team thought that they were "burned" after the second arrest. Still, they stayed at it, mainly because the team wanted to see the rest of the movie. (Cops are not always serious.) On the last one, without too much effort, Deputy Douglas convinced the "lady" that he was an out-of-town insurance agent, in Denver for a meeting. Like many others, when the cuffs were put on, she still did not believe he was a cop. She said "Okay, the jokes over, take these things off and let's get back in bed." Well, the cuffs stayed on and the only bed she got into that night was at the county jail.

Many years later, Deputy Mitch Douglas recalls that the five years in the SCAT Unit was perhaps the most "fun" and productive time in his law enforcement career. Hanging out in strip clubs and massage parlors, with someone else paying for drinks and food, was a difficult job. He is most appreciative that he had the opportunity to serve.

Chapter 6

Domestic Tragedy

Most police officers have lost count of the number of "family beefs" to which they have responded. Calls come in from one of the involved parties, neighbors, passerby, relatives, and so forth. Sometimes cops arrive and no one wants to talk. Sometimes the person who has been assaulted attacks the officers! Years ago, arrests were seldom made unless there was overwhelming evidence of a serious assault. Victims were simply referred to the District Attorney's Office. Domestic violence prevention laws started to be introduced in the early 1980's, mandating arrests. Most cops were glad to see these laws. It gave them a tool that had to be used. Leaving without making an arrest was no longer an option.

Counter to the experience of most officers, Broadmoor Police rarely dealt with domestic disturbances. The Village of Broadmoor residents were generally financially well off. Many were doctors, lawyers, and corporate executives. They were employed in various high-income occupations. These people certainly must have had their share of problems, but they dealt with their issues in a more private and controlled manor. Rarely did the police become involved. When Broadmoor Police did encounter a domestic-related crime, it was an odd occurrence. What follows is in fact a very unusual and bizarre case.

I was the afternoon shift detective working on a quiet Saturday evening. My partner, Sergeant Bret Eddings, had the day shift rotation, and worked Monday through Friday. I worked evenings Tuesday through Saturday. With only Sunday not covered, cases that should have investigative follow up in a timely manner were not likely to be missed. Of course, anything of a priority nature occurring on Sunday would have the office calling one of us at home. It was about 10:00 p.m. and my shift was to end at 11:00 p.m. I was wrapping up the night and sorting through some case files, soon to be off on my "weekend." I had a long list of chores at home to see to.

The call to the Broadmoor Police came in from the Emergency Room at Central Suburban Hospital at 10:04 p.m. The charge nurse told the dispatcher that a man had called, and said his name was Dane Lindsey. He stated that his wife's name was Jenna Lindsey. The man told her that he had called the fire department and was sending Jenna to the hospital in an ambulance, because he had "beaten the hell out of her and pushed her down the stairs." The Broadmoor Police Dispatch lost no time in sending the two Broadmoor police units to the Lindsey home, located on an arterial street on the east side of the Village.

Police and paramedics arrived at the home simultaneously. Dane Lindsey met them at the front door and pointed downstairs. One officer stayed with Lindsey while the other one, accompanied by paramedics, hurried downstairs. They found Jenna Lindsey lying on a bed, completely nude and unconscious. Even the paramedics were shocked at the extent of her injuries. She was covered with bruises and lacerations from head to foot, including all extremities. For the uninitiated, bruises take a few hours to show up. So, it was evident that she had been beaten quite a bit earlier in the day and had been lying there for hours. The officer who went downstairs rushed back upstairs. Seeing the extent to which Dane Lindsey's hands were red and swollen, the officers immediately placed Dane Lindsey under arrest, handcuffed him, advised him of his constitutional rights, and transported him to the Broadmoor Police Station. Upon arrival, he was searched and placed in a cell. As little experience as Broadmoor Police had with domestic violence calls, it was obvious to the officers what had occurred at the Lindsey home.

Jenna Lindsey was transported to Central Suburban Hospital and rushed into the trauma unit. She was comatose, in severe shock, and in overall critical condition. The fact that she was still alive was amazing. I responded to the hospital and spoke with the emergency room charge nurse. She told me that, given these injuries, Jenna Lindsey was not expected to survive. The examination had revealed that she had brain swelling, a collapsed lung, and extreme bruising all over her body. The examination also confirmed that the contusions and lacerations had been inflicted several hours before her arrival at the hospital. Fortunately, it was Jenna's lucky day in that specialist physicians were on duty. A craniectomy was performed by a neurosurgeon to relieve the hematoma that had caused the paralysis of the right side of her body. A tracheotomy was also needed and done.

I telephoned my partner, Sergeant Eddings, and briefed him on the case. He responded directly to the Lindsey home, to coordinate the investigation and supervise a search for evidence. I remained at the hospital, in the unlikely event that Jenna Lindsey would be able to make a statement. After a couple hours, it was evident that there was no possibility that Jenna would be able to say anything at all that night, if ever. I went to the police station and typed up the criminal complaints to be submitted to the State's Attorney's Office. Since Jenna was not expected to survive, I stated the crime in the criminal complaints as Murder.

Sergeant Eddings and his team began the search of the Lindsey house on Eastern Road. It was located on a large lot and backed up to the commuter railroad right- of-way. On one side of the home was an elementary school. On the other side was a utility site. It was not likely that anyone would have been in the vicinity on a weekend, to hear Jenna's screams, if there had been any. Most of the house was in disarray, such as would be left by a violent struggle. The Broadmoor Police Major Investigations Unit had responded and began processing the crime scene. Several rolls of 35mm film were used by the investigators to document the scene. Various items were seized as evidence, including a fireplace poker with dried blood and skin fragments on the business end. These would later prove to have come from Jenna Lindsey.

The Broadmoor Police Major Investigations Unit officers tasked with searching the house were thorough. When a search is made for evidence of the crimes of aggravated battery and attempted murder in a domestic situation, there is a lot of latitude. One of the officers removed a framed photo from the wall and looked on the back. He read a rather strange document. On a sheet of paper was a confession, allegedly signed by Jenna Lindsey, stating that she shot and killed a man by the name of Ivar Rusnick, in his home, in nearby Hazeldell. The statement continued to say that she did this because Rusnick was making unwanted sexual advances to her and would not stop. Further, she stated that she took the rifle used in the crime onto the boat owned by herself and Dane Lindsey and threw it into Lake Michigan while on one of their weekend cruises. The document continued to state that she took full responsibility for this act and that Dane Lindsey had nothing to do with it. Although a bizarre find, the officer rightly entered this document into evidence. This item was not thought about for a few more days since there was the immediate investigation with which to deal.

The next day, Sergeant Eddings conducted a tape-recorded interview with the suspect, Dane Lindsey. Lindsey was advised of his Miranda rights again, and he signed a waiver of these rights. He commented that he might as well get it over with and make a statement, since he could explain what happened. Lindsey said that he and his wife got into an argument Saturday morning. He wanted to have sexual relations with her as they woke up and she said she was too tired, having worked all week. He accused her of continuing what he thought was an affair with a co-worker. She denied this but the argument continued. Lindsey said he lost his temper and slapped her a few times. He said she went into the recreation room and took a handgun from a drawer, and aiming it at him, fired it from several feet away. He said the shot missed and he grabbed a fireplace poker, striking her multiple times. Lindsey said he continued to hit her and pushed her down the basement stairs. At the bottom of the staircase, he hit her head on the floor a few times. He said Jenna lost consciousness and he placed her on a bed. He went back upstairs and fell sleep. Several hours later, he woke up and went downstairs to check on Jenna. Finding her unresponsive, he then called for an ambulance and telephoned Central Suburban Hospital. Next thing he knew, police and paramedics had arrived. Lindsey's hands were still red, and quite swollen, and thus photographs of his hands were taken.

A police stenographer transcribed the tape-recorded conversation, which had begun with Sergeant Eddings advising Lindsey of his constitutional rights, which he had acknowledged and waived. Sergeant Eddings returned to the lock-up and placed the transcription before Lindsey. Lindsey read it and signed it. He asked how his wife was doing. Sergeant Eddings told him that she might not survive. He seemed surprised, which was a little hard to imagine, given the extent of the injuries he had bestowed upon her. These injuries would cause Jenna to remain in a coma for over a month.

The day following the interview, Dane Lindsey was transported to the Cook County Criminal Court Building where he was arraigned at the preliminary hearing on charges of aggravated battery and attempted murder. Judge McKay set bail at $100,000. Lindsey would have to post ten percent of that to secure release. After a few days in the Cook County Jail, he managed to come up with the money by taking a second mortgage against the house that he and Jenna shared. Awaiting a trial that would take place months later, Dane Lindsey was now free, while his wife remained in a coma.

During the following week, the police team looked over the evidence, submitting several items to the Illinois State Police Crime Laboratory. I came across the "signed confession" of the homicide previously mentioned. I wondered if there had been a homicide in the area involving a victim by the name of Ivar Rusnick. I called the detectives at the Hazeldell Police Department and talked with Jim Robinson, a detective whom I knew well. He said the name seemed to ring a bell in connection with a case that the Cook County Sheriff's Department had been working a couple years before. There were quite a few patches of land, dotted with residential areas, in the unincorporated south suburbs. These were not part of any city or village. Crimes committed therein would be investigated by the Cook County Sheriff's Office. I thanked Jim and placed a call to the Detective Division of the Cook County Sheriff's Police Office.

Detective Mike Barger answered. I had not worked much with the Cook County Detectives and was not acquainted with him, but it did not matter. I asked him if he had an unsolved homicide case of a victim named Ivar Rusnick. His momentary silence gave me the answer. Detective Barger confirmed that, about two years ago, Rusnick was shot at close range in his home with a high-powered hunting rifle. Despite untold hours of investigation, they had not developed a viable suspect. I briefed Barger on our case and on the discovery of the "signed confession." Barger said he would meet me at the Broadmoor PD in a half hour. Meanwhile, I made a copy of the document. The original was still a part of the Broadmoor investigation and had to be kept in evidence by Broadmoor Police.

Detective Barger arrived ahead of schedule and read the document. This was the break that they had been waiting for. He had his case file with him. He said that Rusnick had worked at the same large retail discount store where Jenna Lindsey was employed. He had talked to all the coworkers about Rusnick, trying to find out if he had any debts, enemies, or other life problems. In other words, he was trying to establish a motive for murder. Jenna had also been routinely interviewed. Rusnick had lived alone and his body had been found by his landlord, who visited when Rusnick failed to pay his rent on time; he had always paid promptly. Barger noted that the crime scene was quite a mess, due to the use of a high-power hunting rifle at close range. Review of the document suggested there had been some type of a relationship between Jenna Lindsey and Ivar Rusnick that had not been uncovered in the initial investigation. Detective Barger speculated that perhaps the two were having an affair and that Dane Lindsey found out about this and killed Rusnick. Later, Detective Barger interviewed several former co-workers of Jenna Lindsey and Ivar Rusnick and confirmed that there was in fact gossip of an affair. Even as Dane Lindsey was out on bail for what he did to his wife, the investigation of the murder of Ivar Rusnick was reopened, and became a priority with the Cook County Sheriff's Department.

As the parallel investigations continued by the Broadmoor Police Department and the Cook County Sheriff's Office, more was learned about Dane Lindsey. To meet him, one would think of him as friendly and normal. He was the kind of guy with whom you might easily take up a conversation at the local tavern, or in the queue at the grocery store. However, in serious criminal cases, the investigators must learn all they can about the suspect. One never knows when information might be developed relevant to the prosecution.

This information arose in checking Lindsey's background. It turns out that, in the sixties, Dane Lindsey was Officer Dane Lindsey, of the Chicago Police Department. This writer grew up on the south side of

Chicago in that time period. Let me tell you, you did not mess with the Chicago Police. They would kick your butt in a heartbeat, and nothing would ever come of it. Right or wrong, they kept order and respect in those times. Once on the job as a Chicago Police Officer, in that era, it was almost impossible to be fired. Occasionally, some officers would cross the line and be involved as suspects in felonies. (If you think I am kidding, look up "Summerdale Burglars," on an Internet search.) They would be fired and criminally charged. It was unusual, but it happened from time to time. Former Chicago Police Officer Lindsey's file was most interesting. He seemed to have anger control issues as, on numerous occasions, he was drawing and pointing his revolver at people with no real cause. This drew complaints that earned him a few suspensions. Still, he stayed on the job. The "straw that broke the camel's back" was when he pulled his gun on a lippy fifteen-year-old curfew violator and it went off. The youth was fortunate that the bullet only grazed his forearm. Having enough of his antics, Chicago PD sent Lindsey on his way. For unknown reasons, Lindsey was then hired by the local commuter railroad police. He lasted about a month during which the complaints from passengers poured in. Lindsey's police career was over. His superficial friendly side did serve him well in sales jobs, and he held a succession of these up until the time of his arrest.

After three months, Jenna Lindsey was still partially paralyzed and unable to care for herself. She was released from the hospital to the care of her parents, who also lived in a south suburb. She was confined to a wheelchair and was undergoing rehabilitation. Her prognosis was uncertain. She had trouble speaking, but her words could be understood if one listened with care. Her parents had outfitted Jenna's old bedroom at the rear of their home with special furnishings to accommodate her needs. Jenna had met with the lead prosecutor, Charles Lansky, of the Cook County State's Attorney's Office Violent Crimes Unit, and was, with some difficulty, able to give a full statement as to what had occurred on the day she was beaten nearly to death. Concurrently, she gave a statement regarding the murder of Ivar Rusnick. She was there when her husband pulled the trigger on the high-powered hunting rifle. The typed confession found at the scene when she had been beaten was signed by her under duress, as Dane Lindsey subjected her at that time to a beating only somewhat less intense than the latest one. After her meeting with the prosecutors, all was going well until, one night at about 2:00 a.m., someone hurled a Molotov Cocktail at the rear of the house. This was right where Jenna slept. Fortunately, the flash woke Jenna, who called out as a wall of flames erupted. Her parents quickly got her out of the inferno and called the fire department, whose fast response saved the occupants and the house. Not so coincidently, Dane Lindsey was stopped by local police officers for speeding while fleeing the scene. Police quickly put the facts together, and arrested Lindsey for Aggravated Arson and Witness Tampering. At the arraignment the next working court day, the case once more went before Judge Dwight McKay, who ordered Lindsey held without bail.

While in custody for the Aggravated Arson, Dane Lindsey appeared yet again before the honorable Judge McKay. The Cook County Sheriff's Office had completed its investigation and Dane Lindsey was charged with the murder of Ivar Rusnick. Judge McKay again ordered him held without bail on the additional charge. It was apparent that Lindsey was not going anywhere but back to his cell at the Cook County Jail.

In the ensuing trial, Dane Lindsey was convicted of murder in the Rusnick case and transferred to the State Prison at Joliet, Illinois. He next stood trial in the case where he beat his wife Jenna nearly to death. With labored speech, she testified from her wheelchair at the trial. Not one jury member was without tears. It took less than four hours of deliberation for them to find Lindsey guilty on all counts.

Dane Lindsey went back to prison. He became somewhat of a "jailhouse lawyer," filing several appeals which went nowhere. He was a monster. He died in prison in 2005. There were no mourners.

Chapter 7

A Very Unusual Halloween

I t was blustery Halloween evening in the Chicago suburb of Broadmoor. I reported for work at 4:00 p.m. to my assignment as the afternoon shift detective. Rain was coming down in sheets, and wet leaves were falling from the trees. Irrespective of the weather, Halloween was never a good evening to do follow-up police work. I expected the usual stupidity of Halloween, and I would assist the two patrol units with the typical nuisance calls. Sometimes, my unmarked car could be helpful.

My plan changed dramatically when, at about 6:00 p.m., Broadmoor Police were summoned to the Bank of Illiana, located at the south end of the Village. Mrs. Tompkins was in the bank manager's office and quite distraught. She told the responding patrol officer that a suspect had broken into her home and, not satisfied with the valuables therein, taken her hostage. To buy some time, she suggested that they use her car to drive to the Bank of Illiana, where she would withdraw a large sum of cash and give it to him. She went into the bank and immediately told the teller to call police. It did not take long for the bad guy to figure out that Mrs. Tompkins was not coming back, so he sped away in her big late model Oldsmobile 98 sedan. Broadmoor police arrived, took an initial statement, and brought Mrs. Tompkins back to her home. As the on-duty detective, I was notified and met the patrol officer, and Mrs. Tompkins, at her home.

The Broadmoor Police Department had just formed its very own Major Investigation Unit (MIU). Chief of Police Don Jarton had, for some reason, not liked working with the Cook County Sheriff's Police. County had some knowledgeable and experienced detectives and had helped us many times with crime scene processing and other investigations. But, Chief Jarton had some funny quirks and this was one of them. He was convinced that we could do the work ourselves. As much as I liked the opportunities that this case would present, I also knew that there was no substitute for experience. The Cook County Sheriff's Police Crime Scene Deputies had lots of that. We did not. Nonetheless, this was the Chief's order. I would do my best.

Three other officers and I had received training by attending courses at the State of Illinois Police Training Institute. This training included dusting for fingerprints, photography, and other evidence collection techniques. This case was a big deal. It would call upon every bit of the training that I had received. It was a challenge, but

I felt prepared and ready for the task. I arrived at the scene. I would take the lead on this investigation, as well as become responsible for processing the crime scene.

I sat down with Mrs. Tompkins in her living room to take a more thorough statement. She had poured herself a glass of sherry and slowly sipped it, as she related a harrowing story. Amidst sobs, she told me that she was baking cookies in the kitchen, when she heard some noises that seemed to come from the living room at the other end of the house. When she went down the hall to investigate, she was confronted by a black man armed with a knife, who said to her: "Be quiet or I'll kill you. I want your jewry." (sic) She led him to the master bedroom, where he searched diligently through her jewelry box, dresser drawers, and a cabinet. She said that she really is not the type of woman who collected a lot of expensive jewelry. Since the suspect seemed upset at the lack of potential plunder, she suggested they use her Oldsmobile 98 and drive to the bank, where she would withdraw $5,000 cash and give it to him. He agreed to this, telling her: "Don't try anything funny. I have this knife and I'll use it." Mrs. Tompkins said that, distraught as she was, she took a direct route to the bank. All the while the suspect sat in the front passenger seat and displayed the large chrome-bladed knife. When she drove into the parking lot, she pulled into the first available space. The suspect told her to leave the car running. As she had related to the patrol officer, she went inside the bank and told the teller to call police. It did not take too long for the suspect to figure out that Mrs. Tompkins was not going to return to the car. He slid over to the driver's seat, put the big Oldsmobile 98 in gear, and took off.

I next did a "walk through" of the house with Mrs. Tompkins. As was my custom, I put my hands in my pockets so as not to inadvertently touch any evidence. I asked Mrs. Tompkins to do likewise. She showed me the point at which the suspect had entered the home, described his movements, and pointed out several items that he had handled. My outlook brightened immediately when Mrs. Tompkins stated that the suspect had not worn gloves.

I developed a plan to begin my crime scene processing at the point-of-entry, proceeding through the house in a systematic and thorough manner, following the path that Mrs. Tompkins had indicated. The point-of-entry was a window in a first-floor alcove of the house, hidden by shrubbery. The suspect had removed the screen and pried the window open with a tool. I dusted the window frame area with fingerprint powder and developed latent prints of value on the frame of the screen and on the interior windowsill. Since the window frame could not be removed, these latent prints needed to be "lifted." This is done by carefully placing special clear cellophane tape over the developed fingerprint, then placing the tape on a file card. With black powder, a contrasting white file card is used. The card containing the latent print is labeled, placed into evidence, and can later be compared to a card bearing the full set of the suspect's fingerprints taken when the suspect had been, or would be, arrested. I then photographed the window frame surface, which bore tool marks of the pry-type tool that had been used.

Accompanied by Mrs. Tompkins, I proceeded upstairs to the master bedroom area. She pointed out a file folder that the suspect had handled. After looking in the folder for money and finding none, the suspect had tossed it into a clothes hamper. I dusted the file folder with "magna-powder," a very useful metallic substance designed for checking paper and cardboard items for latent prints. Latent prints are those not visible to the naked eye, but that become visible when processed using the appropriate technique. In any crime, fingerprints can be the most important evidence recovered at the crime scene. (This was before DNA technology had been developed.) As I dusted for prints, I saw several latent prints of value develop, obviously very good ones! I placed cellophane tape over these prints to protect them. There was no need to "lift" the prints, as I took the file folder as evidence. As one of my first major cases, in terms of crime scene processing, I was becoming very optimistic that the Illinois State Police Crime Laboratory would indeed be successful in identifying this bad guy! For our Broadmoor PD Major Investigations Unit, it was important that we end up with a good result, proving that we could do the job. I examined several other items, but none yielded evidence as valuable as the latent prints from the point of entry, and from the file folder. In this case, the crime scene processing consisted only of dusting for latent prints and taking photographs. All along, I explained to Mrs. Tompkins what I was doing, and why I was doing it.

As I was packing up the evidence and my equipment, I told Mrs. Tompkins that I believed we had some very good latent prints and we would next focus on finding a suspect as quickly as possible. She asked if the suspect was likely to return. I replied that it was very unlikely, but that should she hear or see anything suspicious, to call Broadmoor Police right away. I also said that extra patrol of her area would be put on the roll call bulletin sheet. I told her not to be surprised if she saw a patrol car parked in her driveway, as officers might be writing reports or sipping on a coffee while parked there.

I returned to the Broadmoor Police Department and secured the latent prints and three rolls of 35mm film in the evidence vault. These would later be transferred to the Illinois State Crime Laboratory in Joliet, about an hour's drive away. I prepared a teletype message, to be sent to all agencies in a five-state area, containing a suspect description, and information about Mrs. Tompkins' stolen Oldsmobile. While the information was fresh in my mind, I wrote up my supplementary reports and headed for home at 3:00 a.m. There was nothing more that could be done that night. When I awoke late the next morning, I learned that my two daughters had a lot of fun "trick or treating" on our block. Another minor holiday with the kids missed. Their Dad was a cop.

In the 1970's, law enforcement didn't have today's technology of the Automated Fingerprint Identification System (AFIS). We would need to develop a suspect whose inked fingerprints, taken in connection with a prior arrest, would be on file. The latent prints which I had developed at the crime scene would be compared to the inked fingerprints of this person of interest. A match would determine the identity of the suspect. We knew this would happen, but it was just a question of "when," and not "if." The break came about two weeks later.

I was working a weekend "off-duty" security detail at a townhouse construction site in the Village of Broadmoor. There had been numerous thefts from construction sites in the south suburbs. About the only way contractors were able to prevent this was to have on-site security on the weekends. By hiring real police officers within their jurisdiction, the contractor's liability was limited, and they got armed officers who knew what they were doing. At about 4:00 am, dispatch asked me to call into the station. I did so, and learned that a suspect, driving Mrs. Tompkins' Oldsmobile, had been arrested the evening prior in Shady Glen, Illinois, only about twenty minutes from Broadmoor. Since I was not immediately available to pursue this lead, I telephoned my Detective partner, Sgt. Bret Eddings. Bret responded and went to the Shady Glen Police Department to obtain copies of the reports and plan follow up strategy.

This was a good stroke of luck. Sometimes it is unbelievable how stupid these crooks can be. Here, two weeks later, the bad guy was still driving the stolen Oldsmobile. He had been cruising through a well-to-do area of Shady Glen, probably looking for an easy burglary target. The Oldsmobile 98 stalled, and he asked some neighbors for help in jumping the battery. It was likely that the big car had just run out of gas. At the time, Shady Glen was mostly a white, upper middle-class suburb. It was out of the ordinary to see black people, especially young males, cruising about the neighborhood. More importantly, the suspect was not well spoken, nor dressed in a manner that fit with the luxury car. The neighbor was suspicious and called the Shady Glen Police, who responded without delay. The dispatcher had routinely run the license plate through the NCIS (National Crime Information System) and LEDS (Law Enforcement Data System). It came back as a stolen vehicle associated with a home invasion/kidnap. In short order, the suspect, identified as Alexander Jefferies, was in handcuffs, and on his way to the Will County Jail.

Since this all transpired on a weekend, nothing else happened until Monday morning. Then, I and my partner Sergeant Bret Eddings, met at the Broadmoor Police Department at 7:00 a.m. We drove to Joliet and were at the Will County State's Attorney's Office at 8:00 a.m. sharp. The Assistant State's Attorney already had the case notes, and had prepared what was essentially a script, that would guide our testimony at the preliminary hearing where Jefferies would be charged with possession of a stolen vehicle. He knew we were more concerned about the home invasion/kidnapping, but the possession of stolen vehicle case was Will County's case and was theirs to prosecute. Cook County was where the home invasion had occurred, but the arrest with the stolen car was in Will County. Each county had its own system and that was how it worked. Our more serious Broadmoor case would be tried later in Cook County.

Double jeopardy would not be raised as an issue since the criminal charges were different.

The Will County Jail had a facility for a proper "line-up" of suspects. The suspect, Jefferies, had remained in custody. We arranged to bring Mrs. Tompkins to the Will County Jail the next day, to view a line up. She was very hesitant, but we assured her that bright lights would keep the suspect from seeing her. She knew how important this was, so she agreed to go. We arrived at about 10 a.m. and sat in an interview room for about twenty minutes while the line-up was assembled. Mrs. Tompkins did not generally smoke. Yet, she borrowed a total of four cigarettes from a jailer as we waited. There were six black males, 18-28 years old, of average height and build. Jefferies was number four. Mrs. Tompkins picked him without hesitation. Before we left, we picked up a certified copy of Jefferies' fingerprints, to be compared with the latent prints recovered at the crime scene. A match would seal the case. As we drove back to Broadmoor, a much-relieved Mrs. Tompkins asked us what would happen next. We explained that we would request a fingerprint comparison be made by the Illinois State Police Bureau of Identification, which we expected to result in a positive match. The Cook County District Attorney's Office would prepare the Broadmoor case for trial, contact her and us as witnesses, and set a trial date. We made sure she knew that, for all intents and purposes, the investigation phase was successfully completed.

Almost a year later, the case went to trial. Jefferies fired his court appointed attorney and acted in his own defense. It was a straightforward case, with a positive identification made by the victim, and confirmed via multiple fingerprint matches. The fact that Jefferies was acting as his own attorney probably resulted in his being sentenced to twelve years in the Illinois State Penitentiary. A real lawyer might have got him only eight years. He was off the street for quite a spell.

Mrs. Tompkins had guts. She trusted us and accepted our advice as to what to do. Her testimony and identification were crucial to the case. As traumatic as the incident had been to her, she stepped up to the plate one hundred percent. By the time this case went to trial, I had moved to an urban area on the west coast about 2,400 miles away. I was working as a deputy sheriff. The Cook County State's Attorney's Office subpoenaed me to return and give evidence. My testimony was essential. I did this gladly and without any question. Aside from the conviction that followed, there was another event that was very important to me. Mrs. Tompkins sent me a thank-you note. She was a class lady, all the way from offering me a glass of sherry, to thanking me for my work. "To Serve & Protect." Sure, it sounds a bit trite, plastered on many patrol cars all over the USA. But, when I received that note with a personal message, the words "serving and protecting" took on a whole new meaning for me. This was what it was all about. Thank you, Mrs. Tompkins!

Chapter 8

Professional Crooks

V ery seldom do any books, television programs, or films, feature burglars. Burglaries do not create the type of excitement as there is with homicides, armed robberies, hostages, etc. The crook breaks in, steals property, leaves, and, occasionally is caught. This would put most viewers asleep in their armchairs in short order. Years ago, there was a television show called "It Takes a Thief," that aired a series of adventures based upon the life of a sophisticated professional burglar who executed burglaries of a very high dollar amount. But generally, stories featuring burglars are not the fare that executives in the highly competitive television industry are seeking for programs.

Most often cops deal with petty criminals. These types are looking to steal something to fund their next hit of dope. They are not smart. They are opportunistic. However, cops do occasionally encounter some real pros. They are not drug addicts. They may even have nice houses, cars, families, etc. They are generally "connected," and part of organized crime. The trouble is that they earn a living by being professional crooks. They are skilled, smart, and hard to catch.

In the Chicago suburb of Braemar, we occasionally dealt with these folks. As I said, they are smart. They plan their scores very thoroughly. They even go so far as to study the activities of the officers on each shift. Most of the officers employed by smaller departments in the Chicago area have their shift assignments rotating on a set basis. The crooks can monitor their scanners for months, figuring out shift patterns and levels of activity. They prefer to plan a job when the least ambitious group of officers is working. I would bet that, to keep their monitoring interesting, they even conjure up nicknames for officers working in their next target area. How about names like "Dopey, "Batman," Energizer Bunny," etc.? Shifts with a high level of self-initiated activity, such as traffic stops, premise checks, and stops of suspicious pedestrians, are to be avoided. This gives them a greater chance of not being caught.

It was in the late 1970's, and many of Braemar's residents were doctors, lawyers, and high-level corporate executives. Before Christmas season and Passover, Smith's Jewelers was well stocked with very expensive gift items. Watches worth thousands of dollars, and diamond jewelry items selling for far more, were on hand for the wealthy customers, usually male, to buy as gifts for their wives, so that the women could try to "one-up" each other at the next holiday cocktail party.

Such was the seasonal holiday atmosphere at Braemar social events.

The professional crooks knew full well that, during the holiday season, high end jewelers would have their vaults chock full of goodies. Of course, the problem for the crooks was the high-end jewelers also had high-end alarm systems. These professional crooks operated well beyond the "smash and grab" crimes. They planned for every contingency and had experts for each phase of their job. A successful heist took months and months of planning. They did not do armed robberies, because those were crimes against persons and could draw heavy time in the pen. Burglaries were, after all, still only a property crime, even if the haul was large. If caught, burglars did minimal prison time, since there were so many violent criminals ready to occupy any cells made available for them upon release of the property offender.

Thus, a certain gang of thugs, well known to the neighboring City of Chicago Police Department, decided to branch out to the sleepy suburbs. They looked to the wealthier areas and settled on Braemar for a score. The strip mall where Smith's Jewelers was located is on the extreme south end of the suburb, largely bordered at the time by vacant fields. A main road went past the mall, but the stores were set well back off the street. One could drive around the mall since the service road to the rear was paved and used for deliveries. There were rarely any vehicles parked behind or in front of the mall at night. Any vehicles so parked would generally be checked by police. A couple of well positioned lookouts could warn their cohorts of approaching police cars. A quick trip in and out, to drop off anyone or anything, would likely be unnoticed.

Another factor in favor of the crooks was the weather. December in the Midwest is generally cold, and the night of the burglary was no exception. This was a weekday night, so there would be little traffic in the area. As cold as it was, about twelve degrees Fahrenheit, no one would be out window shopping. The likelihood of a passerby seeing anything odd and reporting it to police was nil.

So far, initial planning of the score was easy for the crooks. The next part took quite a bit more effort. As was mentioned before, most suburban police departments had rotating shifts. A cunning crook could listen to a scanner for a few months and figure out who was working, and who had a pattern of sparse self-initiated activity.

In Braemar, each of the three shifts had one sergeant and two officers assigned. Because of days off, usually only two police officers, including at times the sergeant, would be on duty. Sergeants had a working role. In Braemar, the Village was split into two sectors, east and west.

Smith's Jewelers and the strip mall stores were in the west sector. This was not a busy Village on night shift. When assigned to patrol, all of us were coached to, at some time during the night shift, get out of our police cars and physically check the security of businesses in our sector. This included at least those in the strip mall and the downtown area. Even though most businesses had alarm systems, the practice of police officers to physically try the doors and look through the windows was a good one. It was, however, most always an uneventful chore. We always logged these onto our "lie sheets," on which we noted the various activities each of us conducted during our patrol shift. Should there have been a burglary or an act of vandalism, the routine security checks so logged would help narrow down the time of occurrence. Most of us had enough of a sense of pride that, if an incident were reported in the morning, we could at least say we checked the business at a precise time. A side benefit was that a couple foot patrols during night shift would help keep the officer awake and alert.

On this cold winter night, the shift sergeant was on his days off. Sergeant Ray Uldahl always checked the businesses. Anyone listening to a scanner would become familiar with his diligence. There were two officers assigned to his detail. Both were working on this specific night. One of them would usually do the security checks, but he was assigned the east sector on this night. The other officer had a reputation for being, well, shall we say, less than ambitious. We will call him Officer John Doe. There would be long periods when Doe was on nightshift where he did not call in anything. For all anyone knew, Doe may have been asleep. This was likely all taken in by the crooks that were planning the job. This night, Officer Doe was assigned the west sector. Being a bit lazy, all it took was the cold weather to convince Officer Doe not to bother checking the businesses. After all, what crook would be out on such a cold night? No reason to leave his warm patrol car. The closest Officer Doe may have come to checking the stores in the strip mall, was perhaps to have driven by on the main road. He would never have noticed that Smith's Jewelers was completely dark, in that the bulbs for the counter lighting usually left on at night had been removed.

The next obstacle for the gang was to deal with the high-end alarm system at Smith's. Alarm systems generally are wired into the telephone line system. It is not a "do-it-yourself" type project, but with some training, the technical aspects of installing and maintaining an alarm system are not too difficult to master. Just the day before, the alarm system at Smith's Jewelers had been converted from a direct line into the Braemar Police Department to a line into an alarm monitoring company. This was the trend at the time, as the monitoring company could deal with the inevitable false alarms and notifications. The company would notify police only when it seemed necessary. Thus, much police time could be saved. This obstacle was overcome when the alarm company unknowingly hired a technician with ties to organized crime. This technician handled the switch-over and knew exactly which lines in the mall mechanical room were dedicated to Smith's Jewelers.

I think two drawings will help the reader understand how this heist was planned, and why it worked. The drawings are not to scale and yet will help clarify what is to follow.

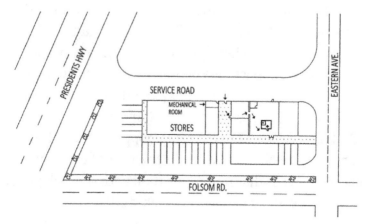

Overall View of the Braemar Commons Mall

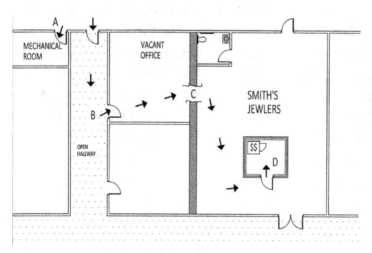

Crime Scene Diagram

Sometime after midnight, the night shift of the Braemar Police Department came on duty. The only business at the Braemar Commons Mall still open was a small restaurant, and as was routine, the owner had finished locking up and was leaving. The criminal gang put their plan into action. They had walkie-talkies to use for communication. They also had police scanners to monitor police activity. Lookouts were posted in inconspicuous places. The alarm technician and another crook with a slide-hammer lock puller were dropped off right at the door to the mechanical room at the rear of the complex. This is "A" in the diagram. The crook with the lock puller screwed the device into the lock and with one slam popped the lock and access was gained to the mechanical room. The corrupt alarm technician took only seconds to hook up wires to bypass the Smith's Jewelers alarm system. The technician remained in the mechanical room and would stay there until the job was completed. His helper meanwhile left the mechanical room and opened a nearby hallway door that was without a lock, walking a few steps into the passageway connecting the front of the mall with the rear service area. He went immediately to a vacant office, marked as "B," at the rear of the passageway and popped that lock with his slide hammer puller. That office shared a concrete block wall with the rear area of Smith's Jewelers. He was then joined by a helper who carried two sledgehammers and gave him one. They worked in tandem to create a hole in the wall big enough to allow the men to enter, along with oxygen and acetylene tanks and cutting torch equipment. This is identified as "C." A panel van dropped off another two men who dragged the equipment in through the access hole. These men set to work with the cutting torch on the large vault in the front of the store, marked as "D." The two men who had created the hole in the wall moved quickly and removed all the under-counter florescent lightbulbs in the front counter/office area. They then used a combination of large blankets arranged to block the bright light created by the cutting torch, which might be visible from the street, as best as was possible. Once the door to the vault was cut open, the "torch team" went to work cutting open the door of the safe which was located within the vault. The extremely expensive items were kept in that safe. As the safe was cut open, another pair of crooks was dropped off at the rear of the complex, with containers into which all the goodies would be stuffed. The crooks were smart in that they could not rely on the men who used the cutting torches to perform other tasks. They had inhaled enough fumes to make it necessary to get them out of there as soon as possible. As the containers were stuffed with jewelry, the other crooks took their tools and equipment out through the access hole, tossing these items into a nondescript panel van. That vehicle left the premises and another similar one took its place. In an instant, the crooks with the loot came out and tossed everything in this second van as they jumped inside. The alarm tech pulled his jumper wires at about 8:10 a.m. and dove into the van just as it was pulling away.

When the alarm technician removed the line jumpers, a line-out signal was transmitted to the alarm monitoring company. These signals were nothing unusual and were often created as a business owner erred in the process of turning off the system upon arrival at work. Routinely, police were sent to check. The day shift had come on duty and Braemar Police Officer Bob Day responded. He approached the front door and gave the handle a shake. It seemed fine and he glanced inside. He was startled at what he saw. The vault door was standing wide open with a pile of debris nearby. He lost no time in calling for cover cars and the on-duty detective, Sergeant Mike Havens.

Sergeant Havens coordinated the response of the Braemar Police Department Major Investigations Unit. The scene was photographed and processed for latent prints. There was evidence that at least one of the crooks, probably a "torch man," used the toilet when he became sick. There was a possibility that he removed his latex gloves in the moment. The toilet seat assembly was removed and taken to the Chicago Police Department Crime Laboratory to process for latent prints, to no avail. Chicago PD wanted to nail these crooks too, as they were very prolific. With the cooperation of Chicago PD, Sergeant Havens pretty much figured out which gang was responsible. There was some confirmation to this theory, as the alarm technician who was a suspect in this burglary died in a suspicious circumstance about two weeks after the caper.

Although at the time this may have been considered a "perfect crime," the luck of the criminal group was to be short lived. Considering the suburbs to be soft targets, they set their sights upon a supermarket in a suburb adjacent to Braemar.

In the late 1970's, many people who shopped at the grocery store still paid in cash. So, by Sunday night at closing, there was a lot of money in the store safe, waiting to be deposited in the bank on Monday morning. The band of thieves figured that they could outfit some trucks with the markings of a roof repair company, and then pretend to go to work repairing the roof of the grocery store. Of course, this was the cover for them to move in, do a rooftop entry, torch the safe, and make off with the cash from the weekend.

This all sounded very plausible and may have worked, but for the alert and inquisitive nature of an Elmwood police officer. Officer John Eddy was patrolling in the area, on this warm spring Sunday evening. He saw the Acme Roofing Company trucks at the Save-More Supermarket. It was around 9:20 p.m., and the market had closed at 6.00 p.m. He saw ladders going up to the roof and a couple of guys up there. Being a former construction worker, Eddy thought it odd for roofers to be on the job on a Sunday night, absent some emergency. He had the Elmwood Police dispatcher call the store manager, who was on their emergency contact list. The store manager knew nothing about it and said there had been no problems with the roof. That was all it took.

The officer requested assistance from the neighboring Braemar and Brentwood Police Departments. The store was surrounded. The store manager responded to the scene and provided a key. The alarm system had been bypassed and the crooks had already lowered the cutting torch equipment through one of the rooftop vents.

Officers entered and a total of six criminals were taken into custody. They were charged and all accepted plea deals. They ended up serving three to eight years in the Illinois State Penitentiary, a fine old building located in Joliet, Illinois. All of these, except for the "replacement" alarm tech, were suspects in the Smith Jewelry case. Fortunately, the Elmwood officer was more attentive to duty than had been his counterpart on the Braemar Police Department.

Chapter 9

Recruit Deputy Jay Parsons' First Day

I t was a beautiful warm and sunny October morning in Washington County, Oregon in 1980. At that time, Washington County was still primarily a rural county. In the eastern part of the county, adjoining the city of Portland, Oregon, young up-and-coming firms such as Tektronix and the fledgling Intel Corporation had established their headquarters. Later years would see a growth in the Washington County high tech industry. Today, Washington County is a smaller version of the "Silicon Valley" in California.

The Washington County Sheriff's Office was the largest and primary law enforcement agency in the County. Small (at the time) cities, such as Tigard, Hillsboro, and Beaverton, had their own police departments. To an aspiring young officer, the County offered opportunity. One could work one's way into the Crime Scene Unit, Detective Division, Traffic, Corrections, or

Administration. Plus, the County had neat western hats that, if you needed to put on your hat for some reason, were quite classy.

In June, the County Board of Supervisors had authorized Sheriff Bud Barnes to hire five more deputies. Two were to replace retirees, and three dedicated to the expanding population and subsequent call load in the eastern part of the county. Matters in the western part of the county generally took care of themselves. The loggers, ranchers, and farmers looked out for themselves and their families. Deputies responded to write the obligatory report, take care of the crime scene, and forward the file to the District Attorney. If a rancher happened to shoot a burglar breaking into his home; that was just the way it was. It would be considered justified, and no more would come of it.

Recruit Deputy Jay Parsons was one of the five new hires. He had just completed the six-week Basic Police Officers Training Program at the Police Training Institute, located in Monmouth, Oregon. Senior Deputy Vince Moore was assigned as his coach. The coach would ensure that the recruit deputy understood and applied not only the Academy training, but also the many Washington County Sheriff's Office procedures. It was the "on the job" practical training that all new deputies needed. There were weekly evaluations to document progress. "Recruit" status lasted one year, a probationary period. Deputies with significant prior experience were not designated as "recruits." They were presented with the regular six-pointed star, as opposed to the five-pointed one that was issued to recruits. If an experienced deputy came from out-of-state, the deputy would attend a two-week course at the academy to become certified in Oregon. They worked with a senior deputy long enough to gain a basic familiarity with procedures at the Sheriff's Office and the geography of the county. Then, being experienced cops, they were on their own. Still, everyone had a one-year term of probation.

Roll call for day shift was at 6:00 a.m. This placed all deputies on the road well before the busy rush hour. More importantly, the deputies who worked graveyard shift could come in and go home, without the late calls that would delay their sleep even further. Senior Deputy Moore and Recruit Deputy Parsons stepped out of the roll call room and walked over to the equipment room, where another senior deputy issued the patrol vehicle keys, hand-held radios, a twelve-gauge shotgun along with five cartridges loaded with "double ought" buckshot (consisting of nine .32 caliber projectiles in each round), and a radar gun if requested. Items issued were recorded by inventory number. Following this, the deputies gathered their briefcases that were full of the forms and small items needed for their work and walked across the street to the lot where then would find their patrol car. They conducted the usual check-over, looking for contraband in the shielded back seat area, checking equipment, and noting any damage. Once all was seen to, it was time to start patrol.

"County 151 to Dispatch, 10-11." Washington County Unit 151 was officially on duty. First came a bit of radar duty on US Highway 26 eastbound at Helvetia Road. During the last year, there had been several fatal collisions at that location. Excessive speed had been determined to increase the severity of the collisions, so some concentrated traffic enforcement was conducted. After writing six citations, all for in excess of 20 mph over the posted speed limit of 55 mph, the deputies stopped at a coffee shop on Northwest 185th Avenue for breakfast.

Their break was cut short as the dispatcher spoke, her voice a bit heightened from the usual day-shift monotone. This was obvious to any deputies listening to their police radios. Shots had been fired within the Washington County Courthouse. A subject was on trial for armed robbery. At the time, there were no metal detectors or screening systems set up for people coming into the courthouse. This was 1980. A female accomplice of the suspect had entered the courtroom and somehow handed the suspect a loaded .38 caliber revolver, and a set of car keys. He let off one shot and bolted out the door. They had it set up as to where the escape vehicle would be parked. In seconds, he was mobile. The suspect drew attention to his vehicle by taking off at high speed, leaving a trail of burning rubber. An alert bystander provided an accurate vehicle description.

Washington County had seven patrol districts with a patrol unit assigned to each. In addition, there were two traffic units, and about a half a dozen detectives on duty. For situations such as this, a "snare plan" was employed. Units would take positions at designated intersections of major roads. The theory was, if a suspect vehicle came through one of these intersections, it would be spotted by a deputy. The vehicle description, a blue early 70's full size GM product, was put on the air.

Patrol Car 151 took up the assigned position at Northwest Cornell Road and Northwest 185th Avenue. Not five minutes later, the suspect vehicle turned from eastbound Cornell to northbound 185th. Senior Deputy Moore put the pedal to the metal, activating lights and siren, and the chase was on. Recruit Deputy Parsons called Dispatch with information that that the suspect vehicle was spotted at their snare post and they were in pursuit, northbound on Northwest 185th from Cornell.

The patrol car was quickly closing the gap. After rush hour, there was not a lot of traffic on Northwest 185th Avenue. Speeds that approached 80 mph were usually considered excessive. However, in the case of pursuing an armed escapee, the high speed was acceptable. At Northwest Springville Road, the road surface for 185th Avenue turned into a dusty gravel surface. Cresting a slight rise at that point, the suspect, hardly an expert driver, lost control and the car spun to a stop and stalled.

Hot on the suspect's tail, Senior Deputy Moore barely had time to avoid a collision as he skidded toward a cloud of dust. He managed to stop and positioned the police car perpendicular to the suspect vehicle about twenty feet away, as the dust settled. He yelled to Recruit Deputy Parsons "Grab the shotgun." Both police car doors were flung open, as the suspect was jumping out of his car, brandishing a handgun in his right hand. The suspect ran around to the rear of his car and faced the deputies as he aimed his handgun toward them. They were the last thing he ever saw.

Recruit Deputy Parsons did not hesitate. From his recent Police Academy studies, he knew that deadly physical force used against an armed escapee was justified. He had also had a lot of practice at the Academy range with a twelve-gauge shotgun. He had jacked a round of 00 Buckshot into the chamber as he jumped out of the patrol car. As he positioned himself next to the windshield pillar, he took aim at the suspect and fired. The suspect went down instantly. As the subsequent autopsy examination revealed, one of the nine .32 caliber pellets hit the suspect dead center in the forehead. Death was instantaneous. On his first day on duty as a Washington County Deputy Sheriff, Deputy Jay Parsons had a most memorable beginning to his law enforcement career.

Chapter 10

A Late Call at Freddie's

I n July 1983, I was hired as a Probationary Police Officer by the City of Portland, Oregon. I was happy yet in a way a little frustrated. I had worked for a department in Illinois for five years as an officer and as a detective. I also served as a deputy sheriff in Oregon for two years, and here I was "on probation" yet again. And, this one was for eighteen months! What else did I need to prove? I knew what I was doing. Still, I was required to go through the entire probationary period. This started off by my working with a "coach," and being evaluated on a weekly basis. I was fortunate in that the Portland Police Training Division, via the precinct sergeants, found coaches who were around my age (thirty-six at the time) who treated me more as an equal than as a "new kid." There is always a lot to learn in a new department, not to mention the geography of a large city. I knew that completing probation would not be an issue. Still you had to prove yourself. For sure, you did not want to come off as a "know it already."

It was yet another typical misty fall day in Portland. Officer Gabe James and I were working dayshift on a busy weekday. East Precinct day shift, on weekdays, was staffed by a preponderance of senior officers. Many of these officers had weekends or part of the weekends off. Most were experienced and capable. Some, however, had a reputation for becoming a bit deaf, especially when it was toward the end of their shift and they were "heading for the barn (the Precinct)." Gabe was not that way. If it was a priority call, we were going. That was fine with me. It was our job.

The call came in toward the end of our shift, just before 4:00 p.m. Darkness was already setting in. Daylight savings time had ended the weekend prior, so night was well on its way. We were at 50th and East Burnside, about three blocks from the precinct. The radio crackled and the dispatcher said "Fred Meyer Corporate Office, 2662 S.E. 21st Street, fraud suspects there now. "720?" The officer working 720 was apparently more interested in going off shift than in doing his job. No response. Any fraud call meant a lot of paperwork, and this no doubt heightened his loss of hearing. Gabe was driving and glanced at me, saying "Looks like we're going." I picked up the mike and responded: "660, we'll go, from 50 & Burn, no cover, we're two-man." Dispatch acknowledged and off we went. There was a pretty good distance to cover, along with wet streets and early rush hour traffic. Gabe was an expert driver and we arrived in as good a time as anyone could do.

We pulled up in front of Fred Meyer Corporate Headquarters. It was a large, older building that had seen better days, just south of S.E. Division Street on 21st Avenue. One of the Fred Meyer security managers met us at the front door. We were quickly briefed on the situation. Freddie's security officers were all plain clothes, and very capable. The Security Division office was on the second floor and had few windows, so the suspects had no idea that police had arrived. The suspects, one male and a female, had tried to make a purchase at one of the Fred Meyer stores with a stolen credit card. They became nervous for some reason and left the store. They mistakenly left an altered driver's license, showing a photo of the male suspect, with the clerk. Fred Meyer Security had received a call from the male suspect, wanting to pick up the license. Security wanted the suspect to come to their offices, so they could call police. They told the suspect to come to the corporate headquarters, since the driver's license was now at that location. The suspects were anxious to retrieve that altered photo I.D. They were desperate. Both the male and the female showed up.

We went up the stairs and through two sets of doors. As we entered the office, we saw the male standing at the reception desk with his back toward me, in an animated discussion with one of the male plain-clothes security officers. The security officer who had led us upstairs gestured to the right and told us "she's sitting over in the interview room." Gabe went into the adjacent room, just a few feet away, to deal with the female. I approached the male from behind, and as I began to speak to him, he turned around just enough to see I was a uniformed cop.

There is a saying used by police that describes jittery, nervous suspect behavior: "Hinkey." Well, he started acting real "hinkey," and began to ease his left hand into his left coat pocket. I had this sixth sense feeling that comes with years of police experience that he just might be going for a weapon. I quickly grabbed his left forearm, and a Fred Meyer security officer grabbed his right. Freddie's security officers were well trained and sharp. I quickly patted the outside of the jacket pocket and felt a hard object. It could only be one thing. I yelled "gun!" Gabe came flying out of the side office, jumping over a table, and we quickly had the bad guy cuffed and on the floor. I reached in his pocket and retrieved a loaded .38 revolver. Additional security officers had already moved in and were holding onto the female suspect. We now handcuffed her as well.

We found a set of car keys in the male's other coat pocket, and located their car parked at the curb outside. Upon opening the trunk, we found all sorts of suspected stolen merchandise and identity theft-related items. We contacted the fraud detectives at headquarters. Two of them responded from the downtown office and set to work helping us sort it all out. We transported the suspects to the detective division for interviews, which was procedure for felony arrests. We did our paperwork there. Detectives had found a motel key in the car for a local low rent motel. They obtained a search warrant and found more identity altering equipment in the room. A quantity of items purchased on stolen credit cards was also found.

I gave this case no further thought until a few weeks later, when I was subpoenaed to court to testify at a "motion to suppress" hearing. One of the local defense lawyers, a former deputy district attorney, was representing the bad guy, and tried to establish that my pat down, search, and recovery of the gun was improper. I testified as to what had occurred and the judge agreed I did have the basis to think the suspect was going for a weapon. So, all charges stood. We had an air-tight case, and both suspects agreed to a plea bargain, through their attorney, with the Multnomah County District Attorney's Office. That week, my evaluation was golden.

Author's note: Not long after I had written this chapter, I learned via the "Police Retirees Network" that Gabe James had been diagnosed with an inoperable brain tumor. His days were numbered. An e-mail address for his wife was provided. I sent her a copy of this chapter along with a note, expressing hope that he would like the story. I said that I really enjoyed my days working with Gabe. She wrote back to me that Gabe was surprised that I remembered him, and that he smiled as she read him the story. A few weeks later, Gabe passed away. I thank God that I had the opportunity to bring a smile to his face, if only but for a short time.

Chapter 11

Acceptance

I n a police career, there are a lot of routine calls and contacts, most of which are forgotten in short order. Sometimes, events that an officer does not even think about are significant to someone else, especially to his or her peers.

I was working nights at North Precinct after my latest training transfer. I had completed about a year of my eighteen-month probationary period. North had a reputation as being a place you were sent if you were a bit too aggressive for the other precincts. It worked out well, because a more assertive approach was often necessary at North. I think the downtown brass thought of us as the "Bad Boys."

North Precinct covered considerable diverse geography. There was the "Avenue District," which included many bars, after-hours houses, and drug dealing places. Then there was the industrial area, all closed at night, but ripe for professional burglars. Then, we had the St. John's District, a lower middle-class working community. There were lots of family beefs and bar fights in St. John's. Rarely was there an excessive force complaint from a St. John's resident. If the hapless recipient of police force received a thumping, he generally knew he had it coming. North Nights officers did not take any backtalk. We just took care of business.

As stated above, my stop at North Nights was during my probationary tour of eighteen months. I had completed six months at East Precinct and another six months at Traffic Division. I was transferred to North Precinct as per the usual rotation. I was quite happy because I had been looking forward to a night shift assignment at a busy precinct.

On this summer night, I was assigned to a beat in the St. John's neighborhood. It was a warm, comfortable night. People spilled out of the bars at about 2:00 a.m. Most of them were highly intoxicated. I got a radio call of a "drunk disturbing" in the lobby of an apartment building on North Lombard Street. This was a very routine call. A couple of cover officers were assigned to assist, since the drunks in St. John's usually liked to fight with the police.

It was my call. In police procedure, if it is "your call," you are the lead and make the decisions as to what occurs. I arrived, and my cover officers were right behind me. I found the subject in the apartment lobby, cursing at no one in particular. I approached him, and from a safe distance of about five feet, said "Hey, buddy, you have to settle down, you're waking everyone up." He faced me and took a defiant fighting stance, saying: "I'm gonna kick your ass!"

That was all it took. In police training, we learned to take the initiative and respond to a threat and not wait for the threat to turn into action. There is no telling what the person has planned or what he is capable of doing. With my left hand, I grasped my night stick firmly and it came like a shot right out of the ring on my belt. Thrusting it forward, I hit him dead center in the chest with the end of the stick, taking the wind out of him. I followed up by grasping the stick high and low and thrusting it at him cross chest. He went down like a brick. In an instant, I had him cuffed and was hustling him to my police car. All by myself. My cover officers only had to watch. He was going to the drunk tank.

I did not think any more about this. After all, it was a very routine call. About twenty years later, I met up with Neal, an officer from the old North Nights Squad, who had been with me on that call. We were at a retirement celebration for another officer. He described that call and asked if I remembered it. I said that yes, very vaguely, I did. He told me that he wanted to tell that story at my retirement. I asked him why, saying that it was not any big deal. He said, oh, yes, it was. Neal told me that the North Night Shift officers were very close. They knew I was a new guy who had worked in the Chicago area. They thought I would probably be okay, but they were not sure. I was untested. Neal said than when they saw the guy take a fighting stance, and then saw me react and drop him in an instant, they knew I'd fit right into the St. Johns detail, and all would be well. To me, it was just a routine call and I took care of it. Cops need to know what each other is made of. It is all about trust. Lives depend upon it. Acceptance came, and I did not even know it.

Chapter 12

The Juvenile Enforcement Unit

The Portland Police Bureau had a new Police Chief in 1984. Tavern-owner turned elected Mayor, Bud Clark, took a bold step and appointed Captain Penny Harrington as Portland's first female police chief. She was well respected and liked as the East Precinct Captain, and virtually all members of the Portland Police Bureau were looking forward to good things happening.

One of the new Chief's first actions was to address the rising number of residential burglaries. She firmly believed that most Portland residential burglaries were committed by juveniles. To combat this, she established a juvenile enforcement unit. Day shift would focus on truancy, and evening shift would focus on curfew. This innovative strategy would reduce the number of young people on the streets and thus reduce the number of burglaries. Both shifts would handle other juvenile matters as needed. Of course, there remained the staffing issue. "Where do the bodies come from?" The Portland Police Association was the official bargaining agent for Portland Police officers and sergeants. The PPA had just won a binding arbitration case for wage increases; something not seen for a few years. Mayor Clark was not happy about this, and sixteen police officers were laid off apparently to make his point. Since Bud had told Chief Harrington that she could not hire more officers due to budget matters, she had to draw the juvenile unit staffing from somewhere. She dissolved the Drugs and Vice Division! Doing away with this unit provided her with sixteen officers, two sergeants, a lieutenant, and a captain! This was just what she needed to staff the new unit. Many officers shook their heads in disbelief. It seemed obvious to any cop that a strong drug unit was needed to focus on the longer term and bigger drug investigations. However, Chief Harrington figured that the precincts could deal with the drug issues. Several significant unrelated events followed, and Penny's tenure as Chief of Police sadly did not last much longer. However, that is another story.

I was fortunate in that, right after my eighteen-month probationary period, I applied for, and was assigned to, day shift of the traffic division. It was very unusual for an officer right off probation to be so appointed. Nearly all officers went right to a precinct at the end of their probation. The seniority system almost always meant that they would be assigned to night shift. My prior experience with other agencies, a real interest in traffic, and a good performance in the Traffic Division during my training rotation may have made this unusual transfer happen. A big plus was that I was able to dodge the usual assignment to nights.

However, the new juvenile enforcement unit was recruiting. The perks of a 4/10 shift (A work week consisted of four ten-hour workdays.), evening hours, SMT off, and plainclothes, was too much to resist. Prior experience working with youth as a teacher made me an attractive candidate. I may have been a bit presumptuous to request a transfer from one choice unit to another, yet I was selected as one of the new members. The brand-new unit took a bit of time to establish itself and work as a team. Partners were assigned and changed. Getting to know one of my co-workers named Dave, I learned he too had grown up in Chicago. We partnered up. Both of us wanted to do a bit more than just scoop up miscreants for curfew violations, and we soon found our niche. It was juvenile prostitution.

In the mid-eighties, many low-life characters had not yet entered the drug trade, which was becoming dominated by evolving "street gangs." Especially in certain areas, being a pimp was viewed by some as a worthy career. Most had a few girls in their "stables," and the vehicle of choice was a Cadillac a few years old. Some of the younger ones did not have a car and we called them "popcorn pimps."

Dave and I worked the high vice areas, looking out for juvenile females on the streets. Usually the girls were run-aways. Some were from Portland and the surrounding suburbs, and others were from farther away. Our job was to take these kids into custody and then to the juvenile detention facility. From the detention facility, they would be returned home. If we could charge them with a crime, we would. That would provide more leverage for the juvenile system. Our sergeants were often a bit miffed with us. We would be tied up on some prostitution deal when the rest of the unit was doing some type of (stupid by comparison, in our view) curfew detail. However, they soon came to understand that we were not just goofing off and we had the custody reports, known as "blue sheets," to prove it. Moreover, we had built up relationships of trust with several social service agencies. This is no small feat for police officers.

Our best and most memorable case came together as the result of an unusual set of circumstances. One early summer evening we were checking the high vice area of lower East Burnside Street. It was still daylight. Streetwalkers often frequented the area. We knew who belonged and who did not and did a quick U turn as we spotted two girls, obviously no more than 13 or 14, in "party" attire and hanging around on Burnside. No way did they have any business being there! We pulled our unmarked car over, identified ourselves, and started to get the story.

Mary & Sue were two suburban girls who skipped school that day. For excitement, they took the bus into the city. Downtown, they met "Louie-Lou," a small-time crook who thought running these girls would be some quick easy money. He took them to the store and bought them outfits that would get attention on the street from Johns. He had just given them a quick "how to prostitute" lesson and had moments before dropped them off near where we found them. I am sure he was salivating as he thought of the money that would be rolling in from the perverts who liked young females. In talking with these girls, we knew they were good kids and had no idea of what they were getting mixed up in. We figured they had good families. We did not take them to detention. We took them home.

We explained to the parents of both girls what had gone on. We told them we wanted to follow up and put this pimp in prison if we could. The girls and their families promised to help. We knew we could do this one. Now the investigative police work started.

We put together two identical photo line-ups of six suspects; one photo line-up to show separately to each victim. Procedures required photos of five persons similar in appearance to the suspect, and, of course, the suspect. The photos are mug shots, but only the head/shoulder areas of the body are shown. The booking number and date cannot be shown. This would be considered prejudicial. As far as the victims know, these are just people. No arrests are mentioned. We showed the photo line up to each victim at her home. Each positively identified the photo of "Louie-Lou" as the man who put them out on the street to prostitute, and each girl signed the photo line-up montage. We entered the signed photo line-ups into evidence. This key element was in place.

We talked with the officer who worked the district where we found the girls and had an unbelievable piece of luck. At the same time as we first detained the girls on lower Burnside Street, Officer Brown was issuing a traffic citation to "Louie-Lou" just a block away. This was a key because it placed the suspect in the area. Pimps invariably hang around near their girls, partly to protect their investment from being taken over by other pimps, but mostly to keep them in line and working. After all, the pimp had put out money for the party clothes and wanted a quick return on his investment.

Dave & I knew we had a winner here. Two positive identifications from credible innocent victims, solid support from the two victim's families, and firm evidence that placed the suspect right in the area, would come together and make this case. We took this to the Detective Division and ran the case by one of the detectives. We figured we had put it altogether for them and they could finish it off, covering the bases that experience has shown to be important in building a strong case. We were not prepared for what happened next.

The detective whom we briefed basically told us these cases were not worth pursuing. He went on about victims ending up not testifying. He did not seem to care much about our input. Thus, detectives were not interested. We were as much as told this would be a waste of their time. We were both disgusted. We handed them a great case, on a silver platter, and they just wanted to kiss it off. We were disgusted, but not without hope.

Dave had some contacts in the Multnomah County District Attorney's Office. We went over and met with Mary Williams, one of the Deputy District Attorneys. She liked our case and took it on. A warrant was issued for "Louie-Lou" and he was arrested. After his arrest, he was transported to the Detective Division as per procedure. Now the detectives had to get involved. Louie-Lou made a statement. As with many of these types, they think they are so slick that they can talk their way out of a corner. His account of his whereabouts at the time in question conflicted with the evidence we had from Officer Brown. We had him!

The case never went to trial. On the advice of his court-appointed attorney, "Louie-Lou" pled guilty to two counts of Compelling Prostitution. With the facts of the case, and the age and credibility of the victims, there would almost certainly be a conviction. That could result in 10 years in the penitentiary. Judges, nor juries, have any use for these creeps that prey on young children. He thought three years on a plea was a far better choice.

Dave & I felt good about this one. At last we were able to put away a real predator. Unfortunately, our own unit did not see fit to recognize us with any kind of commendation. Seems the powers-that-be were more interested in scooping kids up for curfew violations. No matter. We knew we did our job. Additionally, so did the Multnomah County District Attorney's Office. We received a formal commendation, in writing, from the Office of the District Attorney. Dave & I were both all too aware that we had saved two innocent young girls from falling into a deep, dark hole, from which they might never have recovered. Many years later, I think about this case as probably the most important case in my thirty-one-year police career. Without question, it made a difference in the lives of two young girls.

Chapter 13

Routine Call Goes Pear-Shaped.

I t was a typical drizzly Sunday afternoon during the winter in Portland. Temperatures rarely dropped to the point of causing snowfall and yet were cool enough to keep people inside. North Precinct early afternoon shift roll call was at 3:00 p.m. The bigger late afternoon shift started at 4:00 p.m. Early shift provided police coverage during shift change between day shift and afternoon shift. If not for this planned overlap, there would be no police officers on the street at all during shift change. One might get away with this in a small suburb, but not in a large city. Early afternoon shift was thin, and today even thinner. I usually worked by myself, but today was assigned a partner. Scott was an officer I sort of knew but did not generally partner with. Over a few months, I had worked around him off and on. Our styles and personalities were not at all similar and I preferred to work alone or with someone I knew well and trusted. However, on this day I did not have much basis for complaining about my assigned partner to the sergeant. So, off we went in the patrol car to cover the entire precinct during shift change. This was the late 1980's in Portland. If something big was to happen, a police shooting, a homicide, etc., it would probably happen in North Precinct. Having said that, it was a Sunday and wintertime, so it would likely be a routine shift.

On most winter Sunday afternoons, the first stop for an early afternoon shift officer was for coffee. Radio would not give you anything but a priority call until late relief came out. Today there was only our two-man car to call, so that was doubly true. If more officers were needed during this hour, help would have to come from another precinct. We started to head over to a coffee shop near our area of assignment.

This plan was put aside as we received a call that was coded as a priority matter, and yet was nothing exciting to us. Meet Mrs. Jones at 2121 NE Alberta Street, at a pay phone. Mrs. Jones reported that her adult daughter, living at home, had been doing drugs all night, had threatened family members, and would not leave the house. All in all, it sounded like a very routine call for Northeast Portland. It was raining when we arrived, and I told Scott to stay in the car. I talked to Mrs. Jones, a nice older black lady, in the shelter of a doorway. She related that her daughter, Crystal, had been on a methadone program, but had done some drugs during the night. Crystal was threatening other family members in the house. She wanted Crystal out. She then told us Crystal was paying rent at the house and living there with her sixty-two-year old blind husband. I figured that Crystal was just into this old guy for his social security check, and thus put two and two together. I told Mrs. Jones that, since Crystal was paying rent, we legally could not just make her leave the house. Under the Oregon Landlord/Tenant Act, she had tenancy rights. People like Mrs. Jones need our help, and I really tried to avoid just telling them "there's nothing we can do." Although that might be true, it is not what the public expects to hear from the police. So, I told her we would talk with Crystal and see if we could get things to settle down. Quite often, that strategy does have a positive effect. I asked Mrs. Jones to meet us at the house, which was just around the corner. I got back in the car and filled Scott in on what Mrs. Jones told me.

We drove around the corner and met Mrs. Jones in front of her house. I asked her to stay on the sidewalk. Like many houses in that area, this house was on a raised foundation, so that we had to walk up about a dozen stairs to reach the front door. I knocked loudly. A voice inside, whom we figured must be Crystal, yelled "Who's there?" I yelled "It's the police, Crystal. We need to talk with you." She yelled back, "I'm not going nowhere. I pays rent here." [sic] Then, we heard sounds indicating to us that she was beginning to stack furniture to barricade the door.

So much for our routine call. I went down the front stairs to inform Mrs. Jones as to what was happening. I told her that the only way we were going to be able to deal with Crystal was to force the door. I knew that there was not a criminal case here but, what the heck, it was not my door. Mrs. Jones said, yes, it was okay to force the door. So, force the door we did. We were totally unprepared for what happened next.

The layout of this house was typical of many older homes, built in the 1920's, in Northeast Portland. The front door was located on the far-right side of the front porch. Just inside the front door was a foyer. Once inside, on the right was a staircase going upstairs. To the left was the living room, with a dining room just to the rear. A kitchen was just beyond that. Crystal was at the far end of the living room, about twenty feet from where we stood in the foyer. She was standing in front of the fireplace behind her scrawny, blind, elderly husband, who was still clad in his bathrobe. She was holding him up with one arm and holding a butcher knife to his throat with the other. I cursed under my breath. Now we had a hostage incident. I could feel the sweat forming and running down my back under the bullet resistant vest.

I had recently read some books on dealing with hostage situations. I knew that you did not want to just rush in. You had to work on encouraging the hostage taker to talk with you. I had no idea about what Scott was doing, as I was completely focused on what unfolding in front of me. Crystal was still behind her husband, with only her head visible. I did not draw my weapon, because I did not feel that I could fire without endangering the life of the hostage. Moreover, I wanted to establish communications with Crystal. I only hoped Scott was still positioned on the staircase behind me. From this vantage point, using the banister for a gun rest, he could take a carefully placed head shot at Crystal, if it came to that.

As required by procedure, I requested the hostage negotiation team by radio. Per general orders, the SERT (Special Emergency Response Team) would come along with them. I was intent on resolving this myself, but knew I had better ask for the specialists, so that my tactics would not later be questioned should this develop into a police shooting. I thought that this was a very realistic potential outcome. I asked for more officers, and radio rounded one up a total of one from East Precinct. On arrival I saw this was Jack, a cop I knew and trusted. He stayed outside with Mrs. Jones, as I requested.

Meanwhile, I seemed to have established a dialogue with Crystal. She kept making sawing motions with the knife across her husband's throat. A lot of our conversation was typical, telling her it was not worth it, telling her not to harm him, etc. I finally reached the point of asking her what it would take to get her to put down the knife. She finally told me that if her mother gave her some rent money back, she would put down the knife and leave.

I told her I would see what I could do. I poked my head out the front door and asked Jack to see how much money Mrs. Jones had on her. She had $100 in twenties. I took the money and went back in, fanning it out in my hand. I told Crystal that she could have this $100 if she put the knife down and I laid the money down in the middle of the living room floor. I think that I struck a nerve here. She no doubt began to envision the quantity of drugs that she could score for that money. Crystal ran over to pick up the money and did put the knife down. In a flash we grabbed her and handcuffed her. The hostage team and SERT were cancelled.

This was before the domestic violence laws had been enacted, and I felt the best way to keep Crystal out of circulation for a day or two was to place a mental hold upon her. She had clearly demonstrated that she was a danger to others. Boy, she was mad when she found this out. She had no fear of the prospect of jail; but wanted nothing to do with the psyche ward at the local hospital. So, that is where she went. I gave the money back to Mrs. Jones and explained to her that we nearly had to shoot her daughter. She was surprised. I told her I was glad we did not. And I meant it.

I talked with Scott afterward. I asked him what he was doing when I was negotiating with Crystal. He said that he had just watched from the staircase. I asked him if he did not have his handgun out, keeping a sight picture, in case it came to that. He said he did not even have it out of the holster. I made a mental note not to work with Scott in the future.

I thought I did a damn good job on this call. But, as often the case, no commendation ever came about. Well, it is only a piece of paper anyway. In police work, a routine call can go pear shaped in an instant.

Chapter 14

Knocking on Doors Pays Off

I t is funny how some unexpected calls happen on Sunday nights. Absent an unusual event, Sunday evenings are generally quite slow. I was working a beat in North Portland when I was assigned an armed robbery call at the Winchell's Doughnut Shop. You may quip that this would be implausible since cops are always there, but not many of us ever stopped at that location.

On arrival, I took the basic description of the suspect and put it out on the air: White male, 19-25, about 5'5" tall, slender, light color hair, dark jacket, jeans. The two young female clerks said they would recognize the suspect if they saw him again. I began checking the local bars. Often a crook will duck into one for an hour or two until the cops leave the area. No luck. There were a couple "low rent" type motels in the immediate area, so I thought I would check those as well.

I pulled into the driveway of the Portlandia Motel, only a few blocks away. I entered the office and rang the desk bell, summoning the owner from his living quarters behind the office area. I recited the description of the armed robber and asked him if he had any guests that fit the description. He thought for a moment and told me it that sounded a lot like the guy in room twelve. I called for a cover car. In fact, two cover cars.

We made up the usual type of plan for contacting suspects inside a building. One officer covered the window of room twelve on the backside of the motel. Another cop and I knocked on the door. You always stand to the side of the door just in case someone inside gets the bright idea of letting go a few rounds through the door. I have been to crime scenes where that has happened. If the officer had not been off to the side, he would have been shot. A man opened the door. I could see a woman standing behind him. No problems at this point. The guy fit the general description; but then there was nothing terribly unique about that. We told them why we were there and of course said they had been in the room for the past few hours.

I figured we could sort this out quickly enough if the two victims, the girls from Winchell's, could come to the motel and see if they could identify this guy. The way law and procedure were, you could not just load the suspect into a police car and take him to the victim's location. That would be too prejudicial. Unless the suspect was under arrest, you would conduct a "show-up." You detained the suspect for a reasonable time and brought the victims and/or witnesses to the location and had them view the suspect. I got hold of our shift supervisor, Sergeant John Finch. Sergeant Finch was a great sergeant. He knew what to do, made good decisions, and stood up for his officers. I liked working for him. Sergeant Finch found a couple of police officers, in separate cars, to go pick up the victims. When they arrived, we had the spotlight of a police car directed toward an area in the parking lot where we would bring the suspect. We told the suspect that we needed to have some witnesses come and see him. To this point, he was cooperative.

Into the area lit up by the spotlight we took the suspect. With no hesitation, both victims independently picked our guy as the armed robber. The victims had been separated at the "show-up," so that one identification, or lack thereof, would not taint the other person's decision as to the identity of the suspect. I advised the suspect of his Miranda Rights and handcuffed him. He gave us consent to search the motel room and we found a home-made pistol. It was not exactly as the victims described the weapon; but often people unfamiliar with guns cannot provide a very accurate description of them. As scared as the girls must have been, I can understand this.

Procedure was to transport a suspect arrested for a felony to the Detective Division, where he would be formally interviewed. The interview would be recorded, transcribed, and logged as evidence. While this was going on, the arresting officer would do the needed reports, secure evidence, and attend to any other aspects of the case that needed to be done. It was a good feeling to make an armed robbery arrest just a couple hours after the crime had occurred. This case went to trial and the suspect still proclaimed his innocence. Two victims identified the suspect and a similar gun was found in his motel room. There was no scientific physical evidence. Did he really do it? Sometimes eyewitnesses can be mistaken. To convict, it requires that a jury find him guilty beyond a reasonable doubt. They did. He went to prison. That is the way the system works. I received a written commendation for this one.

Chapter 15

April Fools!

This book is full of serious chapters. Occasionally, I think I need to throw in a funny story to lighten it up a bit. If you are a former or present cop, you will probably get it. If not, I hope you get it as well.

It was in the early '90s and I had served my first three years as a sergeant in Portland, Oregon, at North Precinct, night shift. It was a 4/10 (four ten-hour shifts) work schedule, so that was good. The officers and fellow supervisors were great, so that was a plus. However, it was time for a change. I wanted hours that were a bit better, and some different scenery. Thus, I did a little "homework." I found that I had enough seniority to transfer and pull "E Shift" at East Precinct. This shift ran from 6:00 p.m. to 4:00 a.m. I could have Sunday, Monday, & Tuesday off! Perfect! I talked with an E Shift sergeant, "Dr. John," whom I knew well and respected. "Dr. John" encouraged me to proceed. I then talked with the shift lieutenant to be sure it was okay if I came over. That is a common courtesy. If I would be upsetting something, I did not want him coming down on me. All was good.

My transfer came through toward the end of March. I packed up the contents of my locker at North and got situated at East Precinct. About a week into the shift I was learning about the officers on my shift, and they were learning about me. In any police department, the sergeant is generally the first-line supervisor, and can make life happy or miserable for the troops. The other two shift sergeants and I had the same philosophy: we should do all we could for the officers in our charge.

Sergeants made up the daily shift assignments, known as the "line-up." Officers either worked an assigned beat or were "utility." Even the utility officers had preferences as to what part of the precinct they liked to work. Since I had only been at East Precinct a couple of weeks, the officers really did not know me too well. I arrived early at work on Thursday, April 1. It was my turn to construct the "line up" and have a bit of fun on "April Fool's Day." I could not resist the opportunity before me.

I turned the usual "line-up" upside down! Officers who worked in the deep southeast end of the precinct were now slated to work in the extreme northwest sector, and so on. A couple of officers wandered into the sergeant's office before roll call to peer at the lineup. This was normal. They asked me about their assignments. One said, "Sarge, I usually work 770. I see I'm in 620." I replied "Well, too bad, I've got it made up and I'm not going to change it." Meanwhile, I had a second lineup in the drawer, which scheduled everyone where they liked to work.

For my non-police readers, I need to do a bit of explaining. Most officers have patrol districts where they prefer to work on a regular basis. They know the troublemakers in their district and know the officers who work in adjoining districts. An overlap shift, such as our "E-Shift," involves our officers working around officers from afternoon and graveyard shifts. Officers thus build up important relationships with their co-workers from other shifts. Remember that police work often involves life and death situations. Officers need to be able to work as an effective team to resolve many incidents. Taking officers out of their established working area generally is very unsettling to them and should be avoided. If for some valid reason this becomes necessary, a good supervisor will take the time to explain the reason to each officer who is affected by the change.

I clued the other sergeant in as to what was going on. We walked into the roll call room and I could feel the temperature drop about twenty degrees. All were silent and stone-faced. No usual banter. I was facing about a dozen officers, all armed, who, at this moment, did not like me one bit. I read the usual bulletins, notices, and words from the Chief's Office. I read the lineup and you could cut the silence with a knife.

Then, I said "By the way, it's April Fool's Day. Do you want to know where you are really working?" As I read off the real assignments, the roll call room erupted into what I can only describe as a combination of uncontrolled laughter and exaggerated groans! The room thawed out in record time. More important than the funny joke, something seemed to click between myself and the troops at that roll call. Maybe it was that we all could have a good laugh together?

I spent about another four years at "E Shift East," and enjoyed that time. We had a great group of officers and worked the peak hours. We had lots of adventures and interesting calls. The sergeant's job there was really a good one.

Chapter 16

Kenny the Actor

Whenever the issue arises, a certain segment of the population puts forth the idea that prostitution is a "victimless crime" and should be legalized. They wonder why police resources are spent on such harmless activities. It seems many people hold the concept of a prostitute as a good-looking gal, just selling herself by choice as an alternative career. Perhaps this is true of the high-end "call girls," such as those who occasionally gain media attention when a well know politician or corporate executive is found to be purchasing their wares.

Any cop who has even remotely encountered street prostitutes can tell you that prostitution is hardly victimless. The most obvious victims are the women themselves. (Of course, there are male prostitutes, and they are victims as well. Here, however, I will just discuss the women.) A great number of these women have been child abuse victims. Many others have been in situations where they suffered abuse of other kinds. Most of them do not think much of themselves to begin with. Some turn to drugs to escape the horrible memories of abuse by their assailants. In most cases, these were relatives and/or family friends. Often their mothers knew what was going on and denied it. Sometimes the mothers even forced them into situations which were not healthy. What results, in many cases, is the women end up as street prostitutes. Most are managed by a "pimp," who, like a leech, lives off their earnings. Should a girl get "out-of-pocket," she receives a good beating to remind her of who her boss is. Any large city police department will have "mug shots" on file. A real education can be gained by looking at a series of photos over time, taken of a woman working the street. Typically, the first mug shot is of an attractive young woman. You see it and wonder why she is doing what she does. Remember, if her head is messed up from abuse, the looks are not a factor. The life on the street, and particularly on the drugs, takes a toll. The mug shots, over a period of several years, progress to the image of a woman who is wrinkled, missing teeth, and looks decades older than her true age. You see the latest photos and wonder who would ever pay this person. They do. Now, it is just a few dollars. There is quite a reaction from anyone viewing a woman's mug shots comparing the first and the last images. Even in locales where prostitution is legal, rest assured many of these women are but simple tools of biker gangs and the like.

Other victims include law abiding citizens. Women simply waiting at a bus stop in a high vice area are constantly approached by "Johns," who drive past, looking them up and down, asking: "how much?" If you are a man, would you like your wife or girlfriend encountering this daily? If you are a woman, would you like to have this happening to you every day? I think not. Property owners in the high vice areas are also victims, often finding hypodermic needles and sex paraphernalia on the streets, on their lawns, and in the parking lots. One might call these "Quality of Life" issues. Thus, prostitution activities hardly are "victimless."

Besides general attention, as time permits, by the beat officer, most police departments conduct periodic "prostitution missions." The concept is quite simple, either the customers (Johns), or the working women are targeted. The easiest targets are the Johns. Most of them are quite stupid. The prostitute decoys are female police officers.

In setting up a mission, the safety of the female decoy officer is of the utmost importance. She will NEVER get in a vehicle. There are normally "spotter" officers, who will of course watch for safety of the decoy, and wait for a pre-arranged signal from her that the John offered her money for a sex act. Certain rules are followed to avoid an "entrapment" defense sure to be raised later in court by the "John." There will be a paddy wagon or marked police units hidden nearby ready to transport arrestees to jail. You might think it would be embarrassing for female offices to dress up "like that." Well, most times they do not have to expose a lot of flesh. Most street prostitutes are dressed just like anyone else. It is the high vice location, the loitering, and the eye contact, that gives the Johns the idea that here is a prostitute to approach.

I was involved with, or close to, numerous prostitution missions. Sometimes the facts are such that even experienced officers shake their heads in disbelief. In one mission, the female officer serving as a decoy was Sandi. She was tall, early twenties, long blond hair, perfect teeth, and in short, a very attractive woman. To top it off, for the mission, and by her own choosing, she wore a short skirt and high-heeled boots. The mission was being conducted on S.E. Grant Avenue, an area where the cheaper street sex trade workers were to be found.

You would think that the average "John" might see her and pause to think, "Humm. She is too good looking to be here. Maybe she is a cop?" But no. These guys did illegal turns and nearly crashed into each other in order to drive up and proposition Sandi. I think she set a record for arrests that evening. I remember one of the arrestees saying "Yes, I thought she might be an officer. But the chance that she wasn't was too good to pass up." That is the way some of those guys thought.

Another memorable mission was conducted further out on the east side. One "John" was driving a semi, with a fully loaded trailer. Our written orders called for the vehicle driven by the John to be impounded upon arrest. To date, this was generally cars, pickup trucks, vans, etc. I was the Precinct Lieutenant on duty that night, and the sergeant in charge of the mission asked me what he should do. My answer was easy. We impounded the semi, trailer and all. The "John" had some explaining to do to the company for which he worked. The towing bill was significant. That was the first time Portland Police impounded a semi in a prostitution mission!

So, the reader is probably wondering, when will he or she learn about Kenny the Actor? Let me explain. Kenny was a Portland Police Officer who certainly did not look like a cop. He was about 5'8" and thin, late twenties with prematurely thinning hair. He was smart, with a university degree. At university, he had studied acting and performed in various plays. If you tried to guess his occupation by his appearance, you would probably say he was an accountant or a computer software engineer and certainly not a cop.

The vice officer, at Kenny's precinct of assignment, had an idea. He knew of Kenny's acting ability. The plan was to use Kenny as a "John" to arrest prostitutes. The fact that Kenny did not look like a cop was a good start. Fine, but usually the experienced sex trade workers want the "John" to expose himself, or let them grab his penis, to "prove" he was not a cop. The Portland Police procedures were to avoid this. The plan was refined, in that Kenny would assume the character of a "deaf and mute" person, who could not speak properly, and could not hear. No problem for an experienced actor! A camper van was secured. The uniformed vice officer, Ryan, would hide behind the curtains to the rear of the front seats. Kenny had a pad of paper to communicate with the women. When the deal was struck, Ryan would emerge from the rear area of the van and the prostitute would be handcuffed and arrested.

The plan worked better than had been expected. The "deaf and mute" routine completely distracted the street prostitutes, and they never bothered trying to touch Kenny or asking him to show himself. Kenny obviously enjoyed getting into character. He pointed repeatedly at the pad of paper. He talked and mumbled, but his words were hard for anyone to understand. The women made their offers of sex acts in loud, clear voices, and some even wrote down the sex act and price on the pad of paper that Kenny had offered them! Of course, this was seized in each case and became evidence. A huge number of arrests were made that night. Word spread quickly on the street about what the police were doing. It would be a while before that ruse could be used again. Still, it was brilliant, and was quite the talk of the Police Bureau for a long time.

I have another story, but it will not appear here. It is a real success story that involves a young girl who got out of the life with the help of some caring police officers. As much as I enjoy sharing the police world with the readers, I would never take the risk of involving someone that, no matter how much I changed the details, could be seriously hurt by the content. I will just end on this note. A street prostitute is a person. They are someone's daughter. Maybe a parent is part of the problem. They are very much a victim, they need to have our understanding, and they should be offered any available social services. Never condemn them, or think you are so much better than they are. You have no idea what these women may have been through in their lives.

Chapter 17

You Cannot Reason with a Drunk

As many stories in this book have made references to typical damp, misty days and nights during the Portland fall and winter seasons, summers are quite the opposite. It is not uncommon to go for weeks without rain. There is a lot of sunshine. Although temperatures above ninety are unusual, they do occur now and then. However, the humidity is quite low and at night, temperatures cool off and nights are very comfortable. Graveyard shift for police during the Portland summers is really a great gig; providing you manage somehow to get your sleep during the daytime.

It was on such an August night when Officer Erica Drake received a radio call to the Woodside Tavern, in her district, at about 1:00 a.m. A subject, whom tavern staff thought had consumed enough to drink, was becoming belligerent and would not leave. The Woodside Tavern was a friendly neighborhood gathering place on Woodside Boulevard. Both the owners and patrons of the Woodside had no use for troublemakers. Within a couple blocks were all the usual retail businesses found in a community center. We never had calls to this tavern. Never. It was well run, and just did not attract problem people. So, as Officer Drake's sergeant, the call got my attention.

As a street sergeant, it was part of my job to drop by on calls and support my officers. Some calls did not sound right, so I would be sure to drop by those. Of course, the hot calls, like hostages, armed robberies, etc., always demanded that a sergeant respond. There is a fine line walked by a street sergeant in any department. You want to be supportive of your officers, but do not want them to feel like you do not trust them, or that you MUST supervise. Now, there are some officers who never want to see a sergeant at a call. Well, those are the breaks. Sometimes I just showed up. I think that during my patrol sergeant days, I struck this balance well.

Responding to the Woodside Tavern, Officer Drake, accompanied by two cover officers and myself, arrived. As is customary, we all grouped and went inside as one. You never want to go into a call haphazardly, i.e. one by one. A lot of calls are resolved by what we call "mere presence." In a call like at the Woodside, four uniformed coppers coming in, ready to take care of business, should be intimidating. That was the idea. As we walked in the front door the subject of the call was obvious. There he was, standing by the bar, alone, staring at us, with a pint of beer in hand. All eyes were fixed on him. The tavern suddenly became very quiet. It seemed that we were not intimidating enough. Another fine line is that sergeants should generally avoid taking over a call. However, I had a sense about this guy. It just was something about his gaze, his smirk, and his posture, that said that he would not go willingly. As an experienced cop, you just get a "feeling" at these calls. So, I jumped the unwritten protocol and approached him, saying something to the effect of "Hey, buddy, it's time to go." He responded by saying something like "Says who?" Well, I knew the fight would be on. So did Officer Drake. We did not even have to look at each other. We just knew. Instantly we each sprang forward as if on cue and grabbed an arm, the pint went flying, and in the blink of an eye, we had the belligerent drunk on the floor and handcuffed. We did not even need help from our two cover officers.

The best part was, the entire tavern patronage, about 40-50 strong, gave us a standing round of applause. They did not want that idiot there. They liked the Portland Police. We were called, we responded, and we took care of business. No backtalk. We delivered. Sure, it was a small incident. But, that night, I was proud of my officers, and proud to be a Portland cop!

Chapter 18

Good Morning, Vietnam!

I n the mid 1980's, there was a great influx of Southeast Asian refugees to the City of Portland, Oregon. Most of them settled in the near northeast area. One huge older apartment complex, known as Halsey Square, soon became entirely populated by southeast Asians.

Nearby, quite a few small businesses had been established by the Vietnamese and other south-east Asian nationalities. The people that ran these stores worked very hard and were realizing the "American Dream." They had opportunities that were never available in their home countries. One of these businesses was a restaurant called Dza Thong. It had seating for about fifty people and was frequented by many of the Southeast Asian community. Some Portlanders who just liked good healthy food dined there as well. In fact, I used to go there quite often, on my days off, for a good dinner. I was quite familiar with Dza Thong.

This was in the Southeast Precinct area. I was, at the time, an "E" Relief Sergeant. "E" Relief was a 6:00 p.m. to 4:00 a.m. shift whose mission was to cover the heavy call periods. This was especially true on Friday and Saturday nights. I was having a 2:00 a.m. coffee stop at the local Holiday Inn. The motels always liked us to stop by at night. Generally, complimentary coffee and maybe complimentary snacks were to be had. The restaurant, after hours, provided a quiet place to talk with other sergeants and officers. Motels such as the Holiday Inn that had an in-house bar & lounge really liked us to drop in. Any patrons thinking of causing a problem forgot the idea in a hurry when a uniformed officer showed up for coffee. Of course, I always listened to the radio since, as a sergeant, I needed to keep on top of what was happening and be ready to respond to any serious incidents. A lot of officers did not want to involve a supervisor on scene if it was up to them. Nonetheless, early supervisory involvement could often bring about a better result.

Dispatch began to give out a priority call. I could tell by the initial heightened tone of the dispatcher that this was going to be something quite out of the ordinary. "Multiple shots fired, Dza Thong Restaurant, 5055 NE Glisan St. The call-taker heard shots being fired as call came in." To clarify, in large police communications centers, the call-taker takes the call and enters the information into the system. By computer, the call goes to the dispatcher, who gives it out. This results in a quicker response than if one person were trying to do both jobs. My coffee stop abruptly ended. The call was about five minutes away,

"Code 3." On arrival, several officers were already there and had the crime scene contained. Emergency Medical Services (EMS) was just arriving. Lots of people were outside the restaurant. I went in, and saw two subjects, both southeast Asian males in their 20's, lying on the floor on opposite sides of a big round table. Both had multiple gunshot wounds and were literally gurgling and drowning in their own blood. EMS carted them off to Emanuel Hospital, a renowned Trauma Center, where the "unsavable" are often saved. Still, we knew it would likely turn into a double homicide. We put in a call to the Detective Division, and a team of homicide detectives responded to the scene immediately. Meanwhile, some of the officers began canvassing the people outside. All said they either were not there at the time of the shooting or were in the bathroom when the shooting took place. It always amazed me how forty or fifty people could state that they had been in a bathroom which, if "stuffed," could hold only six. Obviously these two shooting victims had a beef and decided to shoot it out. It was sort of like a scene from a saloon gunfight in the legendary American "Wild West."

There is an odd element in this story. At the time, I was taking a community college class on nutrition. I was doing competitive body building in the "Masters" class. To better compete, I thought it a good idea to learn about how food works in the human body. There was a young Vietnamese guy in the class. He was a body builder as well. We chatted a lot. He was a good kid. He was thinking about a police career and even went on a ride along with me. At one point, we talked about the double homicide call. You must realize that the ethnic community of Southeast Asians is very close. A lot of retribution can take place, so people do not talk too much outside their close groups. One day he told me he had some information on that call, from one of his relatives. The info was that the two males had begun arguing over how to split up the proceeds from the sale of stolen car stereos. They settled it in a fatal shoot out. I did not pass this on. There would be no point. The crooks were both dead. No way would I want my friend's relative to get involved. One thing was made very clear to me. Life can be cheap. A few of the Vietnam era army vets whom I know had mentioned this. Now, I understood the concept a little better.

Chapter 19

Thank Heaven for Smokers

I t was another one of those warm summer nights in deep southeast Portland. My assignment there was as an "E Shift" sergeant, 6:00 p.m. to 4:00 a.m. E shift covered the peak call hours, which could be quite busy. We supplemented afternoon shift, which finished at midnight, and night shift, that started when afternoon shift ended. However, this being a weeknight, the call load was light. I met with two officers in my detail at our neighborhood community policing office, in the far southeast area of the precinct. This facility consisted of an older two-bedroom frame house which had been converted for office use. The Multnomah County Parole & Probation officers had one of the former bedrooms for an office, and the Portland Police Neighborhood Response Team had the other one. Staff was generally not there past day shift hours. The former living room had a desk for a volunteer receptionist, and another two desks for officers who might stop by to write their reports. There was also a kitchen, where a fridge, a microwave oven and a coffee pot were located. The fridge usually had a stock of ice cream bars, for which officers would drop "honor" payments into a tin box. Since the precinct was quite a distance to the north, this office was a convenient facility for officers to use. It also provided me with good opportunities to visit and keep in closer contact with my officers. We would often talk about a lot of topics, such as job issues, personal problems, and life in general. Those conversations are important in maintaining an on-going team atmosphere.

"Deep Southeast" was populated primarily by lower income people. It was an interesting mix. Good hard-working citizens, some retirees on limited incomes, and of course the usual burglars, thieves, and drug dealers. As in any police department, certain officers like to work in specific areas. The officers working in deep southeast wanted to be there. Most considered the area to be a "target rich" environment.

Things were quiet at 1:30 a.m. on this typical weeknight, and we had about two hours left before heading toward the precinct to end our shift. I collected a handful of reports while we were talking. I could get a head start on reviewing them so there was less "sergeant work" to do when I went back to the office.

Radio called out "770?" 770 was Officer Erica Drake, one of the officers I was meeting with. She responded and the dispatcher gave out the call. "Suicidal woman is holding a knife to her throat at 5512 S.E. Davis Street. Family members there and she won't put the knife down."

Another officer there was Officer Don Boyle. Don was a real character. His nickname at work was "Opie." He talked slowly and, if you did not know him, you would think he was a country bumpkin. He was far from that. For those readers who are familiar with the television detective "Columbo," that would pretty well describe the persona of "Opie," but wearing a uniform. He was sharp, persistent, and a good cop. He dealt with people fairly and courteously. No one ever called in to complain about Officer "Opie" Boyle.

"Opie" answered up right away "780 will cover." This was the type of call that a sergeant should go to as well, so I answered "3710 going." The Davis Street address was just a few blocks from the Community Policing Office. We jumped in our police cars and arrived in no time.

Parking our police cars a few doors east on Davis Street, we walked to the house, and were met in the front yard by Lester Sims and his teenage son and daughter. He told us that his wife, Melinda, was in the living room. She had a butcher knife which she had raised to her throat and was distraught.

We instructed the family to wait in front of the house next door, and Erica, "Opie," and I approached the front door. Officer Drake called out "Melinda, this is the Portland Police. We'd like to talk with you." Melinda called back "I just can't take it anymore. There's nothing you can do." Officer Drake opened the screen door, and "Opie" stepped inside and moved slowly against the far wall of the living room across from the doorway.

Officer Drake and I remained on the threshold, just barely inside the door.

Melinda was in fact holding a large knife to her throat. She was sitting facing us on a sofa at the far end of the living room, to the left of the front doorway. She told us not to come any closer or she would kill herself. From our training, we knew we needed to attempt to open a dialogue with Melinda. Erica and I did this with the usual questions such as "Why are you doing this?" What are the problems you're dealing with?" Well, Melinda really wanted to talk, which was good. We covered all sorts of issues between her and her family. Both Erica and I related some of our own personal experiences, hoping she would realize that all of us must deal with life issues. At one point, I slowly moved outside and requested radio to have the Hostage Negotiations Team respond. These members had a lot more training in dealing with these situations than we did. It would take them about a half hour at best to respond. I slowly moved back into the doorway and rejoined the conversation. "Opie" was leaning against the wall directly across from the doorway and us. He was saying nothing and appeared to be nearly asleep, as all conversation was between Melinda, Officer Drake, and me. He had slowly managed to get a couple feet closer to Melinda, although he was still a good twelve feet away from her. Otherwise, he may as well have been a statue. I assure you that "Opie" was nowhere near being asleep.

Holding an on-going conversation with a suicidal person, or a hostage taker, is absolutely draining. It is kind of like an argument. They want to do something that you do not want them to do. Imagine yourself having a long argument with a family member. It would exhaust you, wouldn't it? We had been at this for at least forty-five minutes when an officer outside signaled me that the Hostage Negotiation Team had arrived. I again slowly moved outside and briefed the HNT sergeant. He went with me to the doorway and I introduced him to Melinda as another police officer who wanted to help her. Officer Drake and I were both spent and were anxious to hand this off to someone with the specialized training that, we hoped, would be used to keep Melinda from harming herself. "Opie" remained inside, still leaning against the wall opposite the front door. He may as well have been a piece of furniture to any observer. Melinda had paid no attention to him.

In less than a minute, Melinda had told the HNT sergeant that she would not talk with him. She wanted Bob & Erica back. Great. Back we went, once again engaging in a dialogue with Melinda. She seemed like a person who just had no one to talk over her problems with. Until us. She told us she would really like a cigarette. We found one for her, donated by one of the outside officers, and tossed it over to her, along with some matches. She put the cigarette in her mouth; but then needed both hands to strike the match. As she fumbled with the knife and the matches, "Opie" sprang to life! From his pose leaning against the far wall, he yanked his police baton from the ring on his belt and in the blink of an eye, struck Melinda's wrist, causing her to drop the knife. As she yelled in pain, Erica and I rushed in and, along with "Opie," held onto her, removing the weapon from the floor. We had an ambulance standing by outside, and the EMTs brought in a stretcher. Her wrist was probably broken and would be treated in the emergency room prior to her being admitted to the mental health unit. She would go there on a "police hold" since she had demonstrated that she was indeed a danger to herself. Officer Drake rode to the hospital with her in the ambulance. I said to Officer Don Boyle: "Opie, I never saw you move so fast." He replied: "Only when I have to."

Chapter 20

How Dumb Can A Crook Be?

This story is so unbelievable that you will think I made it up. But I did not. I could name the officer involved, if I needed to, and, given access to police records, even track it all down. I was the sergeant on-duty that night. It really did happen this way.

Most cops refer to the 7/11, Plaid Pantry, White Hen, Etc., "Convenience Stores," as "Stop & Robs." The obvious reason for this is that they are as convenient to the crook as they are to the public. Hang around outside and, when there are no customers, just go in and rob the place. The chain stores that are cheap employ only one clerk on duty, so these are an easy score. No matter if the take is just few dollars; it is enough to buy some more drugs.

One night, dispatch broadcast an armed robbery call at one of these stores on S.E. Powell Boulevard. Powell is a main thoroughfare through southeast Portland, and the call was dispatched sometime around 9:00 p.m. It was a typical drizzly, damp winter night in the City. One female clerk was on duty, which made the store an easy target. Most competent crooks know these places just are not worth bothering with. If the clerk follows procedures, there is less than $100 in the till. Still, if you need drugs, whatever amount you take will get you by for a few hours. A doper needing drugs is desperate.

Officer Lender responded and took the victim's statement. This is what he learned. She was working alone when a male, white, twenty years old, slim, about 5'8", with dark hair, entered the store. He walked around but did not pick up any merchandise. He came up to the counter and asked her if she knew anyone who might want to buy his bicycle. She said that, off hand, she did not. He wrote down a "message" phone number for her in case she did find someone interested in the bike. When he left, she tossed the paper in the trash. Lots of sketchy people come into these stores.

An hour or two later, guess who comes back? It is the same goofball, this time telling her he has a knife and wants all the cash. She gives him what was in the till and off he goes. She calls 911. As Officer Lender takes the statement, he has the presence of mind to ask what became of the piece of paper the suspect earlier gave her, with the "message" number for the bicycle for sale. She retrieved it from the rubbish.

Office Lender went back to the precinct with this information. He sat down at the computer and typed in the phone number. He retrieved a person's name, and a list of know associates. He pulled up the mug shots of the known associates and found one who fit the description of the suspect. He put together a photo line-up of six subjects, one of whom was the suspect. He returned to the "stop & rob" and showed the clerk the photo line-up. Without hesitation, she picked the bad guy. Office Lender went to his home address, located him, and placed him under arrest. All of this occurred within the same shift. It really was that simple.

Chapter 21

It Was Only a Scrap of Paper

T his is a story about drug smuggling. At some point, a television documentary about this case was done using professional actors. However, I heard the complete story directly, a couple of years ago, from a very good friend of mine, whom I will refer to as John Lairson. John had just retired honorably from the Oregon State Police as a Senior Trooper. I had not seen the television show, so the story was all new to me.

Most of the Oregon coastline, especially the southern part, is extremely rugged. There are many desolate areas with limited access. It is a prime place for drug smuggling activity. All the smuggler needs are the right contacts and some good equipment. In this case, the equipment involves expensive ocean-going boats.

It was in the pre-dawn hours on a morning in June 1987 that a concerned citizen telephoned the Oregon State Police. The citizen lived in a house perched high on the cliffs overlooking the ocean. He was up early and having a coffee out on his deck. He saw what he thought was a commercial fishing boat in far too close to the shore. He grabbed his binoculars and confirmed what he saw. The boat had no lights displayed, which in and of itself was very suspicious. The citizen thought that lives might be in danger and reported what he saw to the authorities. An Oregon State Trooper was dispatched to investigate. If water rescue resources were needed, the state trooper would summon them.

The trooper knew the area well and took a dirt road that would lead him down to the beach. He came upon a pickup truck that was parked facing him, occupied by a lone male. He questioned the male about what he was doing there and received an implausible story about mechanical troubles with the truck. The trooper did not buy it, and handcuffed the male, placing him in the back seat of the police car. Two other OSP (Oregon State Police) troopers were already on the way, since the investigating trooper had radioed in the suspicious vehicle information when he had come upon it. Upon arrival, one trooper remained with the suspect and the other two troopers walked quietly down the dirt road in the darkness to investigate further.

As they neared the beach, they saw several igloo-style tents and some men dragging large bales from the shoreline to the tents. They saw the commercial fishing boat banging against the rocky shoreline. They radioed for additional police and continued to monitor the activity on the beach.

As dawn was just breaking, additional law enforcement resources had arrived on the scene and police went in with weapons drawn. A US Coast Guard helicopter had arrived, equipped with floodlights, and lit up the beach as if it were daytime. Several suspects were handcuffed and placed under arrest. It was found that these people were in the process of off-loading over eight tons of baled marijuana to be loaded into pickup trucks. The fishing boat had brought in the bales and had come in too close to the rocky shoreline, suffering a ruptured hull. No crew could be found.

As you can imagine, several agencies became involved in this case. Besides the Oregon State Police, there was the US Coast Guard, the Drug Enforcement Administration (DEA), the Coos County Sheriff's Department, and of course US Customs. Crime scene investigators combed the scene for evidence. One of them noticed a small duffel bag near a rock formation. He picked it up and checked out the contents. He found, amongst assorted items, a handwritten note.

The note listed several items concerning boat repairs that must be done, navigation equipment, money needed, and another trip next month. It was signed "Oly." Experienced detectives pursue all possible leads. A veteran detective knows that the slightest bit of information, properly documented and acted upon, can crack a case. The note was taken into evidence and submitted to the Oregon State Police Crime Laboratory for latent print examination. The investigation continued, in hopes of finding suspects higher up in the "food chain" than the flunkies who were arrested on the beach that night.

My friend, John Larison, was part of the investigative team for this case, comprised of several agencies. The team was notified that latent prints of value for identification had been developed from the note bearing the signature "Oly." John was, at the time, assigned to the Oregon State Police Detective Division. Aside from working his other cases, he figured that maybe, with persistence, he could identify "Oly."

By checking Oregon boat registrations, he came up with a name connected with ownership of a sailboat "Elmo's Fire." The owner was listed as one Olaf Jusad. John figured this was an alias in that there were not any other records bearing this name. He knew that oftentimes crooks use an alias not too different from their real name. John started using LEDS (Law Enforcement Data System) to make inquiries. The name Olaf Jusad, with various dates of birth details, was checked over and over in the system. If the information is "close" to the names and birthdates of others in the system, the investigator gets a "hit."

This happened several weeks after Trooper Larison began making numerous LEDS inquiries. The hit gave the name of Olaf Judah, forty years of age. Olaf Judah had one arrest on his record. Twenty-one years before, the then-young "Oly" was arrested in a little town in northern Maine, just after he crossed the border from Canada. US Customs officers had found a marijuana cigarette in one of his socks and turned him over to the police department of the little town on the border. Since this was a criminal offense at the time, Olaf Judah was fingerprinted and photographed.

Trooper John Larison placed a call to the Northpoint, Maine, Police Department. The Chief of Police, the only police officer of the town, answered the phone. John asked the Chief if he still had the fingerprint card and photo of Olaf Judah. After a few minutes of checking files, the Chief said that he did, and agreed to send them. Three days later, the fingerprint card and photo arrived by registered mail. John hand-carried the fingerprint card to the Oregon State Police Identification Unit. Technicians identified the prints on the letter recovered at the crime scene as belonging to Olaf Judah.

This was a huge break in the smuggling case. "Oly" had to be the key man. The investigative team got together and came up with a plan. It seemed "Oly" had his sailboat, "Elmo's Fire," up for sale. A DEA (Drug Enforcement Administration) undercover agent, who had lots of experience with sailing, was assigned to the case. The agent contacted "Oly," posing as simply a guy wanting to buy a sailboat. He made plans to see the boat.

The agent apparently hit it off well with "Oly." The agent hinted that his plans included bringing in "cargo" from south-east Asia. They had a few drinks and "Oly" said that this was why he wanted to sell this boat and buy a larger one. He had plans to bring in a load of hashish next month. At this point, the agent knew that he had a good case going. The US Government provided the agent with the cash to buy the boat. To not buy the boat would arouse "Oly's" suspicions. Besides, buying the boat would allow "Oly" to move ahead with his plans. Also, this would allow the members of the multi-agency task force to move ahead with their plans as well.

"Oly" did in fact buy a larger boat within a week and set sail with his crew for Southeast Asia. He had little to be worried about. He had done this smuggling route many times. The only reason his flunkies got caught last year was because they got too close to shore with the fishing boat and ran aground. It was good planning that his crew on the fishing boat had a "Zodiac" pontoon boat on board and ready to launch, in order to get away from the sinking ship and the shoreline. Besides, bringing in several tons of hashish would be his biggest payload ever. After this one, he could retire to Mexico. Little did he know that his movements were all being very closely followed by the multi-agency investigative task force.

In dealing with large scale international smuggling operations, nations have many resources. These are not the resources that city, county, or even state police can access. When the Drug Enforcement Administration and US Customs are involved, there is a lot of cooperation that takes place between friendly nations. Resources, including Interpol, are there. Suffice it to say that the US Coast Guard and other member units of the team knew exactly when "Oly" and his load departed from southeast Asia. They knew exactly where, in the vast Pacific

Ocean, "Oly's" newest ship, "The Marcola," was located, within a few feet, at any given time.

Several days after The Marcola departed from Southeast Asia, the ship was reported to be approaching the Oregon Coast at about 3:00 a.m. Still in International waters, the US Coast Guard had the authority to board, but only when the subject ship's captain was notified in advance. The plan was to board at night when the Coast Guard ships could approach with lights out. My friend, Trooper John Larison, was aboard one of the Coast Guard ships.

The Coast Guard Ship contacted "Oly" on the radio and asked permission to board. A very much surprised "Oly" denied permission. Of course, this was a Coast Guard formality and the Coast Guard ship moved into a boarding position and would board anyway.

"Oly" knew the game was up and rousted his crew. In a panic, they tried to scuttle the ship. They chopped holes in the hull and, pouring fuel all over, set the ship afire. It was left with the motor running and in gear to help thwart boarding efforts. The crew had donned life jackets and jumped into the sea.

The Coast Guard ship picked up the crew and handcuffed them as soon as they were aboard. Meanwhile, another Coast Guard ship had arrived and, having drawn aside the burning Marcola, retrieved as many bales of hashish as was possible. Just before 8:00 a.m., the Marcola went to the bottom.

"Oly" was pretty cocky indeed, as he sat in the brig on the Coast Guard ship. He told one of the DEA agents "You have no evidence." He was told, "Yes, we saved over thirteen hundred pounds of it. That's enough for a minimum ten-year term in the federal penitentiary." The cockiness faded away.

As if that were not enough, my friend Trooper John Larison next interviewed "Oly." He said, "Oly, do you know why you and I are sitting here right now? Do you know how we identified you? It is all because, one day long ago when you were young and stupid, you got busted for a single marijuana cigarette at the border in Northpoint, Maine. Remember, you were fingerprinted? We found your note left in a bag on the beach where one of your boats crashed. It had your fingerprint on it." At this point, "Oly" just bent over and put his head in his hands.

"Oly's" retirement plans changed from a leisurely life in Mexico, to one of boredom in the Federal Penitentiary at Sheridan, Oregon. If a strong wind came out of the west, he occasionally was able to catch a whiff of salt air.

Chapter 22

Roberta's New Year's Eve

I t was December in Seattle. Cold, gray, and, as usual, damp. In the downtown area near the waterfront, there were numerous flophouses and subsidized living apartments. In years past, these areas in many cities had been referred to as "skid row." Recently, there had been a trend toward "the deinstitutionalization of the mentally ill." This meant those who had previously qualified to live in state-operated housing or asylums were now lodged in the community, via a subsidized living arrangement. They were given drug prescriptions that would maintain them in a state of social compliance. The theory was that they would be able to get along in the community and hold some type of menial job. What really happened was that follow-up by the "mental health professionals" was non-existent or at best sporadic. Once "off their meds," there was no telling how the "clients" might behave. Or misbehave, as the case might be.

On December 31, 2002, at about 2:00 a.m., Officer Roberta Street received a radio call. A resident at one of these subsidized housing apartment buildings was acting out. The subject, John Powers, was a white male, 5'10" and a good 230 pounds. Apparently "off his meds," he was running up and down the second-floor hallway, completely naked, yelling and urinating on the doors to other apartments.

As much as this might shock your senses, it was not a particularly unusual call for this district. All the "mental health professionals" were tucked safely in their beds, probably dreaming of a staff meeting in the morning to mull over the condition of their clients. In the wee hours of the night, the police are often called to deal with the failings of the system. There are many and varied failings.

Officer Street arrived. Her cover officer, Officer Rod Blake, was less than a minute behind. Knowing he would be arriving in short order; she went up the stairs to the second floor and encountered a very agitated John Powers. He was completely naked and ranting out of control. The hallway reeked of urine, and obvious urine was present in a couple doorways. She was unsuccessful in establishing any kind of communication with Powers, and Powers ignored every command Officer Street gave him. She realized Powers needed to be taken into custody and approached him. She knew Officer Blake was only seconds behind her.

The call instantly turned into a real fight as Powers grabbed Officer Street in a bear hug, bashing her head into the wall and creating a large crater in the plasterboard. As this was happening, Powers grabbed at Officer Street's 9mm Glock pistol in her holster. She felt the tug at her belt and caught a glimpse of Power's hand on the gun. As is taught in Portland Police training, she called out "He's getting my gun." Officer Blake was right there and responded. He quickly drew his 9mm Glock pistol and pulled the trigger.

Officer Blake had only a split second to make a life or death decision. If Powers had finished gaining control of Officer Street's handgun, he easily could have shot and killed both officers. There was no time to hesitate. Once again, the police had to bring an end to the unfortunate mess the mental health "system" had created.

Author's note: Many readers will be thinking that matters could have ended in a better manner than the death of John Powers. Maybe. Police are not trained to deal with these situations. A short training course will do nothing to solve the problem. Police must use whatever level of force is needed to save their own lives.

It really all boils down to financial resources. Having a "mental health professional" at home and equipped with a pager does little. The response time, in the wee hours, is a half hour at best and usually longer. Many situations cannot wait. Several innovative police departments have partnered metal health staff with cops. They are in one car and are available over a wide area. There are other approaches as well. This all costs money. Governments need to step up and make this happen. "Defunding police" is not the answer. There are still countless calls to take care of that require sufficient police staffing. The "mental subject off his meds and being violent" calls are not particularly frequent. Yet, they happen.

Having mental health professionals on the street can be likened to maintaining a fire department. Mostly, fire fighters just sit waiting for a call. Is there an alternative? Probably not. Having mental health professionals available for rapid response will save lives. It is the same idea.

Cops do not want to deal with mental subjects. They are not trained to do so. Yet, if they must, and the mental subject threatens their lives, they will rightfully take whatever actions are needed so that they can go home to their families at the end of their shift. You might consider contacting your local politicians and advocating that proper mental health staffing be provided in addition to maintaining police resources.

Chapter 23

Never Lie to Your Mother

The "Pager of Death" went off at about 9:00 a.m. on a Saturday. I was the evening shift sergeant in the Identification Division Crime Scene Unit and on my days off. I supervised the criminalists who processed crime scenes for evidence. I hate to use the term, but it was Portland's "CSI." The day shift sergeant and I took turns for "pager call-out." A supervisor often would be required to respond whenever one of us was not on duty. This weekend it was my turn. I called my pager "The Pager of Death," because when it went off, it was generally a homicide. It usually woke me up in the wee hours of the night on a weekend. That is when people tend to kill each other. They seem to be fueled by alcohol, drugs, emotions, or a combination of these and other factors. This Saturday morning, the beeping of the pager, at an unusual hour, was the beginning of a very strange tale.

As was my procedure, after the pager went off, I telephoned the criminalist who had paged me, to get the story. What he knew was that a woman had arrived for work about 8:15 a.m. at a giant discount supermarket on the east side of the city. She parked in the out-of-the-way employees parking area alongside the building, where employees were directed by management to park. She did not even have a chance to get out of her car. An unknown subject, wearing a ski mask, rode up on a bicycle and stuck a 12-gauge shotgun in her face. I doubt that I need to describe to you what resulted when he pulled the trigger.

Patrol officers had obtained a vague description of the suspect and of the bicycle. There was a rapid transit station not too far away from the crime scene, and an observant officer had found an abandoned bicycle. We took it into evidence as it was possibly related to the crime. We knew that the chance of fingerprint evidence on a bicycle was slim. Of course, with recently developed DNA identification technology there were possibilities, but chances were poor. No matter. This was a homicide investigation, and we would leave no stone unturned.

As my criminalists were attending to the physical evidence side of the case, the homicide detectives were developing their plan and starting what would become a very long day. "The First 48" (hours) is indeed important in any homicide investigation, as stories can change, evidence can be destroyed, and witnesses can fade away, never to be identified and located.

It was obvious that this was not a random act. The victim was targeted. Robbery was an unlikely motive. Even hardened criminals do not go up and blast someone in the face with a shotgun just to rob them. Besides, her purse was untouched, lying right beside her on the front passenger seat. There had to be some connection between the victim and her murderer. As is typical, the first contact for detectives would be the family. Information at the grocery store office provided a name and an address. A detective team went to the listed address, located in a suburb west of Portland. Dwight Bugatti, the Deputy Medical Examiner, went with the detectives, to make the formal death notification.

The house was large and appeared to have been built before the Second World War. The people living there must have held yard sales or sold things at "flea-markets," because there was stuff piled all over the large veranda that went around two sides of the building. It appeared that there had been a large addition made to the home in the past. A somewhat past middle-aged woman answered the door. Detectives and the deputy medical examiner identified themselves and asked if they could come in. A man of about the same age as the woman came into the hallway and everyone went into the kitchen. The occupants of the home were identified as Audrey and Tom Hartley.

It turned out that the victim was the couple's daughter in-law, who had recently moved out due to a pending divorce from their son Ed, who was not at home. Their son and daughter-in-law's child, two-year-old Aaron, was in their care for the day. The daughter-in-law's name was Yuka An, and she was Korean. Ed, Yuka An, and their son Aaron occupied the addition to the house, which was really a totally separate living unit from the main structure. The couple was told that she was the victim of a homicide. Details are never revealed because all of that is confidential in an investigation. The couple appeared to be upset and yet remained stable enough to interview.

Detectives immediately focused upon their son, by the name of Ed. A pending divorce can always provide a motive. He was, according to Mr. and Mrs. Hartley, out somewhere doing errands. They said he had been at home this morning until about 10:00 a.m. Detectives did not buy the alibi but did not question it. Family members often lie for each other. The lies can be dealt with later. The detectives left their cards with the Hartley's and requested that they tell Ed to call them when he returned.

Not too long after the Detectives left, Ed came home. Audrey asked him where he had been early this morning. He said that at about 8:00 a.m. he went up to the usual coffee stand that they patronize to buy a coffee. Audrey asked Ed why he did not bring one back for her as he usually does. Ed told his mother that the stand was closed so he just went on to some stores and did some shopping. Audrey gave Ed the detective's card and told Ed that he needed to call the detectives about Yuka An. Audrey did not say that Yuka An was dead. Some how she felt that Ed already knew. Ed did not say much as he left the house without making the call.

The Hartleys had lied to cover up Ed's earlier absence because he had asked them to do so. At the time, the

Hartleys did not know why. Now they began to wonder if their son Ed had something to do with Yuka An's death.

Audrey had an uneasy feeling about all this. Some call it a mother's "sixth sense." She asked Tom to go up to the coffee stand and to bring her a coffee. She also told him to ask Frank, the owner, what time he opened the stand today. In a few minutes, Tom returned with the coffee. Frank has said that he opened the stand as usual on a Saturday, at 7:00 a.m. Ed had told Audrey that he stopped at 8:00 a.m. and the stand was closed. Audrey and Tom talked about the whole matter and called Detectives Dick Austry and Jack Ryder. Austry and Ryder got into their unmarked car and went right back to the Hartley's.

Back at the Hartley's, Detectives Austry and Ryder sat down with the Hartleys at the kitchen table. Audrey told them the truth; that Ed had left sometime well before 8:00 a.m. and had not returned until after the Detectives prior visit. She said it was Yuka An that wanted the divorce and moved out. Audrey said that Ed was very controlling, and was angry about Yuka An moving out and filing for divorce. The detectives knew this case was coming together, but they were far from done without eyewitness identifications or physical evidence.

As Austry and Ryder were getting up to leave, Tom Hartley said: "Don't leave just yet. There is something you need to know about that has been bothering Audrey and I for years. It is time to get it off our chests, no matter what happens. It is about an unsolved murder that my son was involved with about twelve years ago. However, I want some assurance that Audrey and I won't be charged."

The detectives, somewhat surprised, could sense the opportunity presented to them. They slowly sat back down. However, they could not promise immunity on possible charges. Only the District Attorney's Office could do that. This was explained to the Hartley's and arrangements were made to meet downtown in thirty minutes with the chief deputy district attorney of the unit prosecuting homicide cases. The detectives, and the Hartleys, all got into the unmarked detective car, and proceeded to police headquarters. Being a weekend, the detective division offices were deserted. Recognizing the detectives, the patrol desk officer buzzed them in through the secure door to allow access to the elevators. Chief Deputy District Attorney Perry Wayne was already waiting in the detective division office.

The most bizarre story unfolded. In his single days, Ed was not capable of establishing a steady relationship with females. He clearly wanted them, but there was nothing about him in it for them. So, he turned to street prostitutes in Portland. There was no shortage of them. Union Avenue, Interstate Avenue, Sandy Blvd, and 82nd Avenue were teaming with ladies of the evening. If they were too good looking, they were probably cops on a mission. Streetwise Johns would look for the ones with bad teeth. They were almost always not cops. One night about twelve years before, Ed picked up a street prostitute on one of the "ho strolls." (Streets where the prostitutes congregated.) The usual routine was oral sex in the car for twenty or thirty bucks. This accomplished, Ed wanted more. We can only speculate where the conversation went, and what transpired. At some point, Ed came to the realization that the gal was in fact not a gal, but a cross-dresser. The thought that another male had sexual physical contact with him was more than he could handle. He pulled out his pistol and told his "date" that if he did anything, he would shoot him.

At the time, Ed still lived with his parents Audrey and Thomas, in a rented house in Southeast Portland. They had gone out for the evening, so Ed took his captive there. Ordering him into the basement, he grabbed a twelve-gauge shotgun from a closet on the way downstairs. He did not think twice as he pulled the trigger. This was the only way he could cleanse his soul of what, to him, had been a disgusting homosexual contact.

He had a plastic tarp in the basement and wrapped the body in the tarp. He cleaned up the blood spatter on the walls and floor with a bleach solution. He began to plan his next move. Realizing he was into this murder too deeply, he decided to confide in his parents when they returned home. Audrey and Tom did not like it one bit but wanted to protect their son. After all, no one would be able to trace a street prostitute, even a cross-dresser, to their home. The next day, a six-foot deep hole was dug in the backyard. Neighbors there did not pay much attention to one another, so it was of no concern. That night, the body was lowered into the makeshift grave and covered with earth. The Hartley's lived in the rented house for another couple years. By that time, the grass and weeds had covered up the grisly gravesite.

Chief Deputy District Attorney Perry Wayne prepared a written agreement that, in return for testimony, Audrey and Thomas Hartley would not be prosecuted for the crime of concealing a death by homicide. Both documents were signed and notarized. The Hartleys were transported back home. Detectives set up surveillance on the house. The next day, when Ed returned, he was arrested and charged with the murder of "John Doe," who had disappeared twelve years prior.

The following day, detectives, supported by the Portland Police Bureau Identification Division Crime Scene Unit, Oregon State Police Crime Laboratory personnel, and University of Oregon Archeologists, served a search warrant at the Hartley's former home on Southeast Tollgate Street. The current residents were surprised as the team began the excavation. About six feet down, a blue plastic tarp was discovered. In this tarp were human remains. This was carefully removed to the Multnomah County Morgue where a detailed and scientific examination, documented by photographs, was completed. The examination confirmed the remains were that of a male, killed by a close contact shotgun blast to the torso. Female undergarments were identified. DNA evidence confirmed that the remains were of a person reported missing about twelve years before.

This case ended with a guilty plea and conviction. In the other case, everyone knew Ed Hartley killed his wife. However, there was not enough hard evidence to expect a conviction if he were charged. So, the case of the cross-dresser trumped. Hartley was sentenced to life in prison without possibility of parole. The murder of Yuka An, while never prosecuted, was "exceptionally cleared." Had Ed Hartley not lied to his mother about the coffee stand, both murders could have, to this day, remained unsolved.

Chapter 24

Portland, We Have a Problem

I t was a typical late spring Saturday morning in Portland. Overcast. Most years it seemed that the clouds never went away until after the fourth of July. I was at the gym having a workout at about 10.00 a.m. As one of the Crime Scene Unit Supervisors, I had "pager duty" that weekend. The day shift sergeant and I worked a "4/10" schedule, meaning we worked four ten-hour shifts each work week. We both had had Friday, Saturday, and Sunday off. One us had to be "on call" when neither one of us was on the floor in the unit. On the three-day weekends, that meant one of us was "up" all weekend for any major crime scenes. These included homicides, suspicious deaths, officer-involved shootings, fatal traffic collisions, and other serious incidents where the presence of a supervisor was needed. My criminalists responded to the scenes and did all the on-site forensic work, including photography and the collection of physical evidence. The criminalists also attended the autopsies, performing the same tasks. The crime scene unit sergeants worked closely with the detective division sergeants to ensure that the crime scene was processed properly, leaving no stone unturned.

From time to time, prostitution activities turn into homicides. I think everyone reading this book has heard of the "Green River Killer." A man known as Gary Ridgeway preyed upon prostitutes in the Seattle-Tacoma area in the 1980's. He was eventually caught and linked to scores of homicides. If you have not done so, you really should read the books about these horrible crimes, and how, decades later, Ridgeway was finally linked to the murders, arrested, and successfully prosecuted.

My pager went off while I was on the treadmill. The fact that the pager was activated at about 10:00 a.m. was a bit unusual. I called the office right away and learned the naked body of a woman had been found just off a dead-end road leading onto a hiking path in Forest Park. Forest Park is one of the largest urban forest reserves in the USA, running along a ridge on the west side of Portland. It encompasses over 5,100 acres and has almost seventy miles of hiking trails. It is undeveloped, with lots of old trees. That is just how Portlanders like it. Hardly anything major ever happened in Forest Park. We had the odd illegal campsite, or lost person, but did not have naked bodies dumped anywhere very often, so this was something quite out of the ordinary.

After a quick shower, it took me about twenty minutes to arrive at the scene, close to the industrial area in Northwest Portland. I took a semi-paved narrow road just off the main highway up about a half mile to a wide parking area. People would park there and go off to hike, walk their dog, or jog on some easy trails that started from that lot. I met with Detective Sergeant Dan Burns. The detective team had already interviewed the woman who had discovered the body. She was walking her dog when the dog took an interest in a blackberry patch that was in a depression of land. As the woman went over to see what the dog was investigating, she saw the face-down naked body of a dark-haired woman, probably in her early thirties. She had neither seen nor heard anything unusual. There was no clothing near the body. Condition of the body was good; it had been there mere hours. Detectives were already coordinating a systematic grid search of the area. The area to be searched was cordoned off, and grids established. Each grid would be thoroughly searched. There were leaves, field grass, and all sorts of vegetation in the semi-cleared area. Small items disappear quite easily in such conditions but still, you had to give it all the effort you could. Due to enormity of the task, Portland Police Cadets were called in to assist with the search. One team of detectives began walking the trails leading to and from the scene to search for additional clues.

This team came back in about five minutes, looking more serious than usual. They went right up to Sergeant Burns and said: "Sarge, we have a problem. There is another one about 100 yards up the trail. I immediately said to myself: "Portland, we do have a problem. We have a serial killer."

The second body bore an eerie resemblance to the first body. The woman was tall, medium build, long dark hair, and in her mid-thirties. Her clothing was strewn about in a tight area several feet from her body. As with the first victim, her body condition was good. It was apparent that both victims had been killed and dumped there overnight.

The second body changed the nature and intensity of the investigation. One body, well, homicides do happen. Two bodies, now we have a serial killer. Detectives and criminalists would have to work closely as a team to ensure that all items of possible value as evidence were collected.

I immediately called in a second team of criminalists. Although clearly related, the scenes had to be treated separately. Aside from the great amount of work required in connection with each victim, it made sense to ensure that there was absolutely no possibility of evidence from the first victim being mixed up with and thus contaminating evidence from the second victim. This would be critical at a trial.

After the immediate area was searched, the police cadet unit began to assist with an expanded grid search. We needed a lot of personnel to conduct a complete grid search, and they were a valuable resource. Anything that did not grow there, or was obviously old, would be photographed and taken into evidence.

We had one witness, who had not seen anything that could provide an investigative lead and, we had two dead women without any identification. We needed to identify these women. If they had been arrested, there would be fingerprints on file. The bodies were removed to the Multnomah County Medical Examiner's Office, "The Morgue," where the criminalists took rolled fingerprints from each victim. This is not pleasant work, but it is part of the criminalist's job. Fingerprinting persons who have been burned, or have decayed, is much more unpleasant. At the Identification Division, out of which we worked, the prints were entered into the AFIS (Automated Fingerprint Identification System). If there are "hits," point values are assigned to each "candidate." Usually, the prints belong to the highest scoring candidate. This must be verified by three criminalists, to ensure that mistakes never occur. The identification process is crucial and time sensitive. It gives the detectives a place to start.

"Hits" came back on both victims within several minutes. Each victim's inked "ten-print card" was on file in the office because they had been arrested by Portland Police officers in the past. Criminalists were busy as they made identifications by systematically comparing the prints taken at the morgue to the prints on the inked ten print cards. As per the procedure noted already, the initial identification made by the first criminalist was confirmed by a second criminalist, and then verified by a senior criminalist. In this way, the possibility of an identification error was practically zero. Now that identifications had been made, subsequent record checks revealed a common factor. Both women had recent multiple arrests for prostitution.

The fingerprint identification of the victims was all important and provided clear direction for the homicide team. The prostitution arrest record of the victims was the key to the two homicides. Detectives would check the last known addresses of the victims and see if anyone could help them establish what the two victims were doing in their last hours. Investigators were confident that both victims had been "working," and were picked up by the same killer. It was quickly learned that both victims had indeed been working the street in the "Old Town" area of downtown Portland. A key point noted by the detective team was that both victims had a very similar appearance. Both women were about 30 years of age, were tall in stature, had medium builds, and had long dark hair.

Detectives came up with a plan. They reasoned that the killer would again be looking for another similar victim in the Old Town area. There was no time to lose. They set up a mission, using a female decoy officer who fit the same description as the two murder victims. Most "Johns" approach prostitutes in their cars, not on foot. The detectives would set up a well-planned surveillance. This would include recording license numbers of any cars, and descriptions of their occupants, making any contact or showing any interest at all in the police decoy. The goal was not necessarily to make arrests, but to identify suspects for follow up. Incidental arrests would likely have to be made and patrol division would assign officers to deal with that.

The plan worked. On the first night, a male subject contacted the police decoy. He did not take the bait, but detectives had his vehicle license number and thus hopefully his name. They obtained a mug shot and the decoy positively identified Edward Sampson. One experienced detective, Don Schlage, recalled dealing with Sampson, and Sampson became the prime suspect because he had been recently been arrested in Portland for various sex offenses. This was a key point.

Criminalists had recovered DNA evidence from the victims and submitted it to the crime laboratory. The detectives could not waste time. If Sampson were the killer, immediate action would likely save lives. A detective team picked up Sampson at his place of work. Experienced detectives know that better results are obtained from interviews conducted at a police facility. Interviews at work or at homes are problematic, in that the person has all kinds of excuses about things he or she must do, and thus the interviews often get cut short before detectives can get to the heart of the matter. Sampson was asked to come downtown with them to talk about a case. He agreed and got into the unmarked police car with the team. As is customary to keep a suspect at ease, the detective team made small talk on the fifteen-minute ride to police headquarters. More subtle, and maybe not so subtle, pressure would be applied in the interview room, where there would be no distractions. Detectives already knew that Sampson normally worked swing shift and had taken the night off the same night as the murders occurred. This was brought up early in the interview, and Sampson could not account for his time in terms of what he did. The detectives placed several crime scene photos of the victims on the table in front of Sampson and told him that they had DNA evidence from each body that would be compared to his DNA. Sampson briefly looked at the photos and put his head in his hands. He took a deep breath and said "OK, I did it. The DNA will show it so I might as well tell you what happened." The detectives advised Sampson orally and in writing of his constitutional rights, which he waived. A tape-recorded statement was taken. Sampson was placed under arrest and lodged at the Multnomah County Jail. Search warrants were obtained and executed for Sampson's DNA, and for his vehicle. Evidence obtained confirmed his confession. He pled guilty to the two murder charges and agreed to "life without parole," to avoid a possible death sentence. This was a great investigation, using good basic detective practices. There is no doubt that a quick arrest saved additional lives. Portland Police Detectives really shined in this case!

Chapter 25

A Funny Story

Any police officer desiring to retain his or her sanity needs to be involved with people outside "the job." Some do this with teams, hobbies, service clubs, etc. My way was with a British sports car club. At a monthly meeting, I learned about this police story.

I was talking with a younger couple who had just moved to the United States from England and both were working in the Portland area. Being English, they had recently bought a classic MG. They came to a club meeting to meet others who also enjoyed these automobiles. We will call this fellow Ian. Soon after arriving in the Portland area, Ian was driving his rental car one night along US Highway 26, a busy commuter freeway on the west side of Portland leading out to the suburbs. Ian, as most UK drivers, was accustomed to standard shift and not the automatic shift automobiles that make up American car rental fleets. As he drove along the freeway, his left foot would occasionally end up tapping the brake by accident.

A patrolling deputy from the Washington County Sheriff's Office saw this. Applying the brakes off and on without a reason is often one of the signs of a drunk driver. Thinking perhaps this was the case; the deputy got behind Ian's vehicle and turned on his red and blue overhead lights, making a traffic stop. He walked up to the driver's window and asked Ian for the registration and insurance papers, while also looking for clues to impaired driving, such as an odor of alcoholic beverages, fumbling with identification, and slurred speech. Ian replied that the requested items were "in my boot."

Now, here we get into a language barrier. Many think English is the same world-wide, but it is not. Between countries, and even within countries, some words or expressions have different meanings. In most of the United States, "boot" is a footwear item. In the west, "cowboy" boots are common. Often people tuck a knife or a small gun into their western boots. It is just "the way" out there. However, in England, "boot" refers to what North Americans call the trunk of an automobile.

When Ian told the deputy that his registration and insurance were in his boot, the deputy immediately became suspicious. He thought that maybe this guy is looking for an excuse to grab a knife or gun from his boot. So, the deputy then asks: "Well, what else do you have in your boot?" Ian replied, "Oh, a set of golf clubs and a laptop computer." Convinced Ian was either drunk or being obnoxious, the deputy said: "Maybe you better step out of the car. I've got to see this." Ian stepped out, and the deputy stared at Ian's feet. Ian saw the puzzled look on the deputy's face and suddenly Ian realized what was happening and quickly explained what he meant to the deputy sheriff. Both had a good laugh, and everyone went on their way.

Chapter 26

Is He? Or Isn't He?

I t was one of those typical damp fall Portland evenings in November. There was enough drizzle and mist in the air to keep everything wet, but not bad enough to cause one to run from the car to the house. Portlanders tend to put up with the gray wet winter only because the summers are so good. Police work tends to slow down a little as winter settles in, mostly because people are not out at all hours of the night creating havoc. Still, the crooks are out there looking for an easy score. Most of the petty criminals have some type of a drug habit to feed.

Afternoon shift had been busy handling calls since coming on-duty at 4:00 p.m., and most of those officers were trying to get in a dinner break. A radio call came out about a male trying to cash what seemed, to the cashier on duty, to be a stolen check, at a store on N.E. Glisan Street.

The complainant was a cashier at one of the "money markets" that tend to proliferate in the lower income areas. These businesses make their money by cashing third party checks, and making short term "payday" loans, sometimes even taking car titles as collateral. When there were usury laws, the terms were illegal, and desperate people went to loan sharks. Now, usury is legal, and the customers pay through the nose because of their situations. The less intelligent crooks do not recognize that the people who run these stores are smart and have learned all the tricks that the crooks try to use. The stores have many information resources. The cashiers routinely check with these resources to be confident as possible that the check will be okay, and that the identification is valid. When fraud is suspected, police are called.

It was Officer Melissa Gray's patrol district, and she answered up for the call. Dispatch did not need to assign a cover car, because Officer Terry Mulligan got on the air and volunteered. Officers on a specific shift work around each other every day and take care of each other. A cover car always went on calls like this because officers never knew what the call could turn into.

Officer Gray was (and still is) a good friend of mine. She works out regularly to keep fit for the job. She is a smart, pro-active officer who takes care of business. Her work ethic is beyond reproach. I have always had the greatest respect for Melissa. So, Melissa arrives, parking out of sight around the corner, and enters the store by the only door, right at the front. She knew her cover car was just a block away.

The suspect was at the cashier's window, his back to the door. She saw that he was probably about six feet tall, a good eight inches taller than she. He had on a tan suede jacket and casual pants. He was not a scruffy street person. For some reason, he turned and saw Officer Gray. He suddenly drew a revolver from his waistband. In a split second, Officer Gray's hand moved to draw her weapon and fire. However, she saw what later was found to be a Clackamas County Sheriff's Office badge dangling from the suspect's neck by a chain on a black leather badge holder.

The worst nightmare for a police officer is to shoot another cop. Although this situation did not add up, Officer Gray hesitated for just an instant. This was enough for the suspect to finish bringing up the gun that he had just drawn and aim it at Officer Gray. She no longer had time to draw her own weapon, but thanks to her quick reactions and being in shape, she grabbed his forearm and pushed it upward. He had his finger on the trigger and the gun fired. Fortunately, the bullet went up into the ceiling. Officer Mulligan, seeing what was happening through the windows and hearing the shot as he arrived, came charging in through the door. As the officers knocked the suspect flat on his back and prepared to handcuff him, the gun went flying across the room.

As it turned out, the Clackamas County Deputy Sheriff's badge and identification were stolen a few days earlier.

A deputy's home had been burglarized. The badge and firearm were among the items stolen. The bad guy had a couple checks that he had taken, along with the burglary victim's identification. This crook went to jail and was charged with a whole lot more than a mere fraud offense.

Melissa and I talked about this over a couple pints of ale at the "Horse Brass" Pub—after work of course. This was our favorite watering hole. (The pub is in Southeast Portland and has been there forever. If you are in Portland, Oregon, you really should stop in. It is more British than many pubs in England!) Any cop in her place would have hesitated as well. She was smart enough and quick enough to do what she did. Had she taken time to draw, the bad guy's bullet would have got her. She did exactly the right thing. It is part of why Melissa is a good cop.

Author's Note: Prior to publication, I heard some very sad news. Officer Melissa Gray had been medically retired from the Portland Police Bureau for several years, as a result of duty-related injuries sustained in a fight with a bad guy. She suffered some serious health conditions and had moved to a sunnier climate. She enjoyed riding her motorcycle. We had kept in contact. On February 5, 2017, she unexpectedly passed away, at the age of forty-five. Originally, I had given her a different name in the story. Now, I have used her real name. She was a great cop. Melissa was pro-active, honest, had a solid work ethic, and all in all was everything a cop should be. Using her real name allows me to pay a tribute to her. I attended a Memorial Service for Melissa. One of her Sergeants, who really took a special interest in her well-being when she attempted to come back to work after her duty-related injuries, organized the service. She had no family to speak of, and otherwise may have passed unnoticed. Melissa deserved this service. Thank you, Sergeant Steve, for all the work you did to make it happen. Melissa, you are not forgotten.

Chapter 27

The New Sergeant &
A Quiet Holiday

I t was early on a sunny 4ᵗʰ of July holiday. The weather forecast was for a hot day in Portland, and any beaches along the Columbia River would be crowded with people. Most of these people would be, to one degree or another, under the influence of alcohol or drugs. Sometimes they would become a police problem. Most of the time, day shift on a holiday in Portland was relatively quiet. Afternoon shift, on the fourth of July at Northeast Precinct, had to deal with, among other things, traffic issues and people problems in the area of Interstate 5 and the Columbia River. And of course, in other parts of the Precinct, officers had to deal with the masses that had been altering their state of consciousness all day. Every 4ᵗʰ of July, the City of Vancouver, Washington put on a huge display of fireworks just across the river from Portland that attracted both river and vehicular traffic. Thus, it was a big deal for Portland Police in the evening, but not for me. I was on day shift and should be on my way home by 4:30 p.m., well ahead of the bedlam.

After clearing roll call at 7:00 a.m., and attending to some minor paperwork, it was time to head to the "Coffee Folks" store on N.E. Grand Avenue. Along with me was Sergeant Jennifer Adams. It was her first day on the job at Northeast Precinct as a newly promoted sergeant. I was the senior sergeant at the precinct, and I really felt responsible for helping a new sergeant get started. It is a big transition going from officer to supervisor. You must look at every call and every major incident in an entirely different manner. We took our seats in the empty café. I mentioned to her that day shift at Northeast Precinct was usually very quiet on holidays. A few minutes later I was proven wrong.

The Columbia River is a wide body of water separating the Cities of Portland, Oregon, and Vancouver, Washington. On the East side of the City, the Glenn Jackson Bridge carries I-205 traffic over the River and connects the two cities. Mid-river, and on the Oregon side, was a large piece of land known as Government Island. It was only accessible by boat and all that was on it was brush, trees, and of course beaches. Government Island was not part of the City of Portland. It was under the jurisdiction of the Multnomah County Sheriff's Office. Should police attention be needed, the Sheriff's Office had two well equipped and very fast river patrol boats. Portland Police would always assist if requested.

On holidays such as 4th of July, Government Island attracted a sketchy crowd. Most celebrated with drugs, alcohol, or a combination of these substances. The celebrants generally had no worries about routine police presence, due to the remote location. Many of attendees brought tents and camped for the weekend. There could easily be a couple hundred people there.

Our quiet day ended when radio dispatch called us and said that the Multnomah County Sheriff's Office River Patrol Unit needed our assistance. They had a call of a subject on Government Island threatening people with a rifle. As we cleared the coffee shop and sped toward the County boat launch facility, I requested all but two Northeast Precinct cars to meet myself and Sergeant Adams at the County boat ramp. This was located on NE Marine Drive, at about N.E. 45th Avenue, obviously right on the Columbia River. I had a lot of concern, because there was no cover available for a tactical approach onto the Island, especially from the water. We could call out a police aircraft if need be but, the call belonged to Multnomah County, and, when contacted, the County Sergeant said to hold off on the plane.

At the boat ramp, we split into two groups, one for each Multnomah County River Patrol boat. There were two deputies on each boat, one being a sergeant. One of my officers was a SERT (Special Emergency Response Team) member and had brought along his rifle outfitted with a scope. The SERT officers were highly skilled and trained well. Close was not good enough. They never missed. I was glad to have him there.

Both boats approached the Island from the West. Sergeant Adams' boat landed on the west end of the Island and she led her team as they began walking in at a safe distance from the camping/partying area. Due to the slope of the land, they could hit the sand for some short-term cover if needed. My boat came in further east, adjacent to the camping area, right near shore. We had no idea where in the group the subject with the rifle would be; but we did not see a general panic so that was a good sign.

In any situation like this, you want the subject to come to you. There is no way any supervisor would have officers wade into this group. We formed a plan. My boat was equipped with a public address system. As Sergeant Adams' team neared the encampment area and all officers had taken positions, I made the following announcement:

"This is the police. We know there is a man with a rifle. We do not want anyone to get hurt. We want the man with the rifle to lay it down and walk toward our boat with hands in the air." We all held our breath. There was no telling what would happen.

From one of several tents amidst everyone a man in his twenties emerged and put his hands in the air as he walked toward the boat as told. Sergeant Adams' team took him into custody. They went to his tent and secured the weapon. Sure enough, it was a semi-automatic rifle. We all breathed a huge sigh of relief.

As we learned, the man was a US Army soldier and had recently returned from service in Iraq. Soldiers there always slept with their weapons. Their lives depended on it. This soldier had somehow acquired a similar civilian issue weapon while on leave, and of course he had it in his tent. Apparently, he was tired and could not sleep. Some people outside the tent were making noise and would not leave him alone. His solution was to point the rifle at them. It turned out not to be loaded, but who would know? That is when police were called. After his trip to jail, I have no idea what happened to him. Probably he was turned over to the US Army Military Police.

Sergeant Jennifer Adams, on her very first day and in fact, in her first couple hours as a sergeant, found herself in a potentially very dangerous tactical situation. She showed good leadership skills, sound judgment, and a calm presence under pressure. This was quite a test. At that point, I knew that she would be a great sergeant and a capable leader.

There is a bit of an aside to this story. When Sergeant Adams and I sat down for coffee, she said, in a way that seemed to ask for a response: "You've probably heard about me." I quite truthfully told her that I had not really heard a lot. I never paid a whole lot of attention to Bureau gossip. That was all I said on that point. I did know that she had dealt with some very sensitive and personal matters and resolved them in a manner that was best for her. These matters had nothing at all to do with her integrity as a police officer. I had been a sergeant for fifteen years and had learned to accept many different types of people and ways of doing things. In today's era, this was no different. I would form my opinion as time went on by how she did her job. Nothing else mattered. I expected the officers on our shift to do the same.

At the "man with a rifle call," she did just fine as a leader. As the months passed, I found Sergeant Adams to be one of the most capable sergeants with whom I have ever worked. She earned the respect of her officers. She was good at identifying and dealing with problems. After a time, she took over a precinct street crimes unit that had become quite dysfunctional. She got the unit back on track. She worked with me on addressing some precinct problems that needed help from the street crimes unit. Somewhere along the line, I was serving as a day shift lieutenant and said to her that, if I were ever putting together a team and picking sergeants, she would without a doubt be one of the first on my list. I was very serious. I think that meant a lot to her.

Chapter 28

Sometimes Sergeants Are Appreciated

One nice sunny spring day in Portland, as a Sergeant, I was cruising about the streets of Northeast Precinct. It had been a typical routine day. Suddenly a priority call came out that a student at Grant High School was seen by other students in possession of a handgun. The School Police Division would respond, but meanwhile Northeast Precinct officers would be much closer and thus were dispatched. They would be the first officers on scene. I was close by and it was my area of responsibility anyway.

The police sergeant's job is somewhat unique. The brass up above usually do not spend much, if any, time out on the street. The higher up they go, the more this is true. (A notable exception to this is former Portland Police Chief Charles Moose, who regularly wore his uniform and went out to work a shift with an officer, removing his insignia of rank. In my opinion, he was the best Chief of Police that Portland had in my twenty-four years of service in that city). Sergeants, however, are, or should be, out on the street a lot. Officers are a capable and smart group. They do not usually need to be told what to do, but they do need to know they have the sergeant's support and help. The Sergeant also needs to look at the big picture and anticipate potential "land mines." The sergeant needs to know his or her officers well, in terms of personalities, capabilities, and personal problems that could influence matters at work. A sergeant cannot do that if he or she is not out on the street interacting with the officers as much as possible. It really all amounts to building mutual trust.

Portland Police, as other agencies, had trained, to some degree, for these situations. The first action is to isolate the threat if possible, meaning the student in question. I began quickly thinking over strategies. As the Sergeant covering the area where Grant High was located, I picked up the radio mike and stated I would respond. I ordered that the three cars dispatched to the school be parked out of sight in the service area behind the building. I added that myself and the officers would meet in the main office.

The plan formulated would be for our police team to go to the area of the student's classroom with a school official. The student would be called out of class on a pretense. Once in the hallway, he would be quickly taken into custody. This would prevent any danger to other students. Provided that all remained stable, this plan should work well. Of course, it could all change in a heartbeat.

Should this turn into an "active shooter "scenario, we had all been trained as to how to proceed. A team of five officers would assemble. Positions would include the point officer in front, an officer on each side, a rear guard, and a fifth officer as team captain in the middle. We would determine the locations of the shooter, or shooters, by the sounds of the gunfire. It would be our job to go in after the suspect(s). This tactical plan works very well. Staying outside and surrounding the building was no longer an option.

We arrived and put the first plan into action. The student was called out to proceed to the guidance office. Not knowing whether the gun was on the student's person, one officer was positioned in an adjacent doorway, ready to shoot if need be. He was armed with an AR-15 rifle. One shot, if needed, would end the problem. The area behind where the student would exit the classroom was constructed of concrete block, so bullets would be stopped.

The student emerged and was given orders to put his hands up and drop to the ground. He did exactly as he was told. He was quickly handcuffed and questioned. He told us the gun was a paintball gun and was in his locker. A school official and officer went to his locker and retrieved the paintball gun. The students who reported this did exactly the right thing. Usually one cannot tell these types of weapons from the real item. The student was turned over to school officials. Our job was over.

So, what about Sergeants being appreciated? To begin with, any hot incident, gun at a school, armed robbery, kidnapping, etc., is broadcast on all Portland Police channels, so that all officers on duty know what is unfolding, and are alert in case help from other precincts is needed. Most officers are interested in following what is happening, so they leave their car radio on their assigned channel, while turning the portable radio on their belts to the incident channel.

After the incident was over, I received a message on my MDT (Mobile Data Terminal), the car computer, from Jim, an officer at East Precinct. It was something to the effect of "I heard the call at Grant. It sounded like it could come to something bad. When I heard you come on the air, and give out the plan, I knew it would all be okay."

This type of comment means a lot to sergeants. We need support, too. It felt good to know that Jim, and others, had confidence in me. It reminded me also that Sergeants need to get on the air as soon as they can on hot incidents so that everyone knows a supervisor is on the call and who is in charge, a plan has been made, and the police will be the driving force to resolve the problem. So, thanks Jim! It was always a pleasure to serve with you.

Chapter 29

This Is Air One. Can We Assist?

I t was another sunny summer morning in Portland, close to 11:00 a.m. I was one of the two day-shift sergeants on duty at Northeast Precinct. I was cruising about the Precinct, since all my morning paperwork had been done. It was just a nice time to be driving around and enjoying the day. It was one of those days when I was thinking: "Gosh, I get paid to do this!" I would drop by the odd call to assist my officers or maybe just visit a bit. The other sergeant on duty and I were going to meet for lunch shortly at a little restaurant on Northeast Fremont Street. The "Wing & A Prayer" had a healthy menu, with a lot of items featuring brown rice and chicken. Despite what you might think, most of today's cops are very health conscious. During any given mid-day mealtime, it was normal to find some of us there. A lot of the SERT (Special Emergency Response Team) members ate there as well. Pity the idiot that might come in and try to do an armed robbery at that restaurant!

The radio ("air") was quiet. Years ago, a lot of the public had police scanners. This way, they could hear all the police calls that went out. They listened to everything from robberies in progress to complaints about barking dogs. Every call went out over the air. People could use this free entertainment system in order to keep tabs on what was going on in their neighborhood. Back then, airtime was precious. During peak call times, there was constant air traffic, and the "saturation" level was often over ninety percent in Portland! Officers and the dispatchers had to be concise. In the 1990's, CAD (Computer Assisted Dispatch) came to Portland. Only priority calls which posed an immediate threat to life or property, and thus required an immediate police response, were dispatched by clear voice. Officers, of course, would also call in their traffic stops and other matters such as checking out suspicious persons. Routine calls were sent electronically to the district officer's MDT (Mobile Data Terminal). Officers were expected to check their MDT frequently to make sure they took their lower priority calls within required time limits. Sergeants were responsible for checking their own MDTs and making sure that calls did not sit too long. If a district officer was be expected to be busy on a complicated call for some time, the sergeant would have the call assigned to another unit, or another officer might just use some initiative and pick it up themselves. Following a period of adjustment, this system worked out well. The intended effect of freeing up airtime was achieved. The sale of police scanners decreased substantially.

As I was driving toward the restaurant where the other sergeant and I were going to meet for lunch, the dispatcher's voice on the radio interrupted my thoughts: "East Precinct Unit 992 is pursuing a stolen motorcycle southbound on I-205. Turn to the East channel for more information." I quickly changed to that channel. Our procedures required that, if practical, management of a pursuit should be handed over to a sergeant from the newly involved precinct when the pursuit crossed precinct boundaries. This was because each precinct sergeant knows his or her officers, their capabilities, and the geography of the precinct. Thus, I had to be ready to assume that duty, should the motorcycle enter Northeast Precinct boundaries. In order to prepare for that eventuality, it made sense to learn all I could about the pursuit before the handoff might happen.

As mentioned in an earlier chapter, motorcycle pursuits are usually not worthwhile. Speeds become too great, and officers may take risks that should not be taken. A pursuit is an adrenalin rush, sometimes affecting an officer's judgment. That is one of the reasons that sergeants are tasked with pursuit management. As I listened to the speeds involved, I noted that the pursuit had exited the freeway at Northeast Glisan Street. I figured this pursuit would be terminated by an East Precinct supervisor quite soon.

Then I heard a familiar voice on the radio: "This is Air One. We have an eye on your motorcycle. It is westbound on Northeast Glisan at 60th Avenue. Can we assist?" The East Precinct sergeant replied: "Yes, take over the follow. All ground units, disengage. Patrol units, you may follow the route on parallel streets in a safe manner but stay out of sight of the motorcycle." A key factor here is that now we did not have a pursuit, as defined in the Portland Police General Orders, with all its attendant liability.

Air One is a fixed-wing, single engine aircraft. The crew consists of a pilot and an observer. Some jurisdictions, such as Los Angeles Police, use helicopters. Both types of aircraft have pros and cons. Helicopter maintenance is far more expensive than maintenance of a fixed wing airplane. This is one of the reasons that Portland uses the fixed wing configuration. A big advantage of the fixed wing aircraft is that the plane is very quiet. Air One is used in a lot of "drug follows," and the subject being followed has no idea that police eyes are looking down upon him or her from above. The observer in the aircraft cannot be prone to motion sickness, because there is a lot of circling and intense observation of the subject vehicle, person, or scene.

This was one of those very unusual situations where some good luck had arisen. Air One was not on a specific mission. It was a training flight. Officer Matt Hadley was an experienced pilot. In the seat behind him was Jess Sims, who also had his private pilot's license, but today was serving as an Air One Observer. Obviously, the pilot has a lot to deal with in flying, so the trained eye of the observer is needed for Air One to perform its mission.

Despite the lack of pursuing police cars, the motorcycle driver continued driving in an erratic and dangerous manner. Air One reported that the bike was being driven up on sidewalks, going through red lights, and overall being operated in a reckless fashion. While this was of great concern, there was no longer a "police chase," so police liability was not involved. The police were not pressing the motorcycle driver. The biker had no idea that his movements were being monitored from up above. Patrol units were clearly leaving him alone, and he was still driving recklessly even though he was not being pursued by police.

Air One continued to track the stolen motorcycle as it wound its way, via a circuitous path, through Northeast Portland. It had indeed entered my Precinct and I reiterated the orders "Not to engage. Stay out of sight." A couple officers reported sightings from several blocks away, confirming what Air One had reported as to direction of travel. The motorcycle headed back eastbound and reentered I-205 at Northeast Killingsworth Street. However, this time it headed northbound. It appeared to Air One that the bike would continue across the Glenn Jackson Bridge, crossing the Columbia River into the State of Washington. Per our rules, we could not, under these circumstances, continue the pursuit. However, we would contact Washington authorities. If they engaged, Air One would continue reporting the path of the motorcycle if Washington authorities requested this assistance.

However, there was one problem that cropped up. Portland International Airport is just off the I-205 Freeway. It is a busy place, with huge passenger jets landing and taking off all day. Continuing to follow the motorcycle would cause Air One to fly right into Portland

International's airspace. Pilot Matt Hadley, a very sharp officer himself, wasted no time in contacting the airport control tower and was granted permission to enter the airspace. Departing planes would wait, and incoming aircraft would have to go into a holding pattern. This was great cooperation from the Portland International Airport Control Tower.

Portland International Airport has its own police department, the Port of Portland Police. They have uniformed and plain clothes officers. They dealt with all law enforcement issues at the airport. Therefore, the Port Police were advised of what was happening with the motorcycle. They did not expect to become involved, since it was most likely the motorcycle was going to cross the bridge and enter Washington State.

However, sometimes police matters take a strange twist. Air One reported that the motorcycle exited I-205 and headed west on Airport Way, right toward the airport! Port of Portland Police were put on high alert and ready to take whatever action they could, should the motorcycle enter their property.

Unbelievably, the motorcycle sped right into the multi-story parking garage! Now, this was 2007. Since September 11, 2001, airports in the USA had become the best equipped facilities in terms of video surveillance & monitoring. Airport policing was no longer a job for retired city police officers merely looking for something to do. This was now a job demanding highly trained and professional staff. Some retired city officers were part of the staff, but there were very high expectations of them as well as of newly hired officers. A great deal of training and preparation had been done to deal with potential terrorist activities. Per Standard Operating Procedures (SOP), the Port of Portland police dispatcher instantly put the responding officers on a containment plan for the parking garage. This strategy was one of many designed to cope with terrorist threats. The driver of the stolen motorcycle had no idea of the response he had triggered. In seconds, the vehicle exits were blocked by heavy metal gates, each manned by two officers armed with AR-15 semi-automatic rifles. The two pedestrian access points were closed off and each covered by a team of five officers, with their usual armament plus two AR-15 semi-automatic weapons. You might think this was overkill, but this was the SOP and besides, there was always a chance that this could indeed involve a terrorist plot.

The tactical arrest team of six uniformed Port of Portland police officers rushed to the parking garage as the dispatcher updated all officers on the suspect's actions as seen on the real time video monitors. The suspect was seen dumping the stolen Harley on the second floor, running down a stairway to the first floor, and entering the woman's restroom. In seconds he was yanked out of a stall, handcuffed by the arrest team, and carted off to jail.

A great result was had. No collisions, no injuries, no risk to the public caused by an active pursuit, and another great accomplishment for Air One. The moral to the story: If you are behaving badly, you really do not want to involve the police at any major airport in the USA.

Chapter 30

Check for a Wanted Subject

P olice receive many routine "check for a wanted subject" calls. These involve police officers going to a location, most often a residence, and seeing if the wanted person is there. The first thing an officer does is to obtain a photo of the subject. These can usually be retrieved on the police car's MDT (Mobile Data Terminal). The officer must know what the subject looks like. Otherwise, how does he know if the person who answers the door (if anyone answers the door) could be the one being sought? Most times, they will not confess to the officer that they are the wanted subject!

So, having seen the photo, the assigned officer must find at least one other officer to go along on the "wanted" check. Two other officers are even better. Two can go to the front door, while one covers the obvious escape route at the rear of the premises. Depending on the seriousness of the crime noted on the warrant, and the nature of the place to be checked, additional officers might be a good idea or perhaps even considered essential.

It was a weekday summer afternoon, and Police Officer Tom Clausen received a radio call to check for a suspect wanted for a probation violation. It seems Charles Jones had failed to report to his probation officer. The probation followed a conviction for the crimes of burglary and assault. Nothing too odd here; many probationers just seem to have a hard time remembering these pesky appointments. Officer Clausen would have help from Officer Bill Jacobs, who had volunteered to cover the call.

The address given was in a part of northeast Portland that encompassed an old development of tiny houses that had been known as Vanport. Generally, these houses had only one or two bedrooms. The houses had been cheaply built right after the Second World War to accommodate the recently discharged troops who were starting families. Most of these were now low-end rental units, into which the owners avoided putting any more money than was necessary. Consequently, most of the tenants were either on the somewhat shady side or had friends and relatives who were. A "check for wanted subject" request often comes from a probation officer, as in this case, who has gone through the records and contacts. This often reveals some places where the errant probationer might be "hanging out." Other times, the source of the call to police or the probation officer might be a friend or lover with whom the subject has had a falling out. No matter what the source, police needed to go and check.

Officers Clausen and Jacobs went to the front door. Another officer went to the rear. They knocked and a woman answered. Officer Clausen asked if Jones was there. She replied that he was not. Officer Clausen asked if he could look around and check for Jones. She said that this would be okay. Right then, the officers thought it very likely that the woman might have tipped off the probation officer, having had some issue with Jones. Otherwise, people generally will not let officers stroll through their homes. As the officers opened a bedroom door, there was Jones. Officer Clausen ordered Jones to put his hands up, while Officer Jacobs drew his Taser weapon and pointed it at Jones. Jones dove through an open window just as Officer Jacobs fired the Taser darts. Unfortunately, the darts missed, and off went Jones. This all happened so rapidly that the officer at the rear of the house did not have a chance to nab the fleet-footed suspect.

Officer Clausen grabbed his radio and called for a containment of the area. This old residential development was an easy location at which to set up a police perimeter. Surrounding roads and some natural obstacles provided barriers to escape. Sufficient police officers were close by and not busy, so the area was sealed off quickly. Responding officers did a check of the obvious places where the fleeing subject could have hidden. Officers Clausen and Jacobs were positive that the fugitive was contained somewhere within the police perimeter. Officer Clausen asked dispatch to locate and send a K-9 team.

As the day shift sergeant, I had been monitoring my radio. I already knew what the call was about, as I had followed it on my mobile data terminal. That is one of the tasks sergeants routinely perform. A sergeant always should be aware of what is happening on these types of calls. Circumstances in this call had quickly developed and indicated a sergeant should respond to help coordinate the search for the bad guy. I knew that the area was well contained and that a canine unit was responding. All sounded good so far.

K-9 Officer Adams, and his pure-bred German Shepard "Bismark" arrived. Police dogs are a great tool, their sense of smell is 800 times better than that of a human! There is a lot to working with these animals. You have to be aware that, when the K-9 has found a "hot" track," the dog and handler are quite focused. Sometimes the scent of the suspect is so strong that it pools and drifts. The K-9 team can thus "overshoot" a place where a bad guy may be hiding. Therefore, it is essential that another two officers, and perhaps an "arrest team," run with the K-9 officer and his dog.

The K-9 team and the two assisting officers started the track at the house from which the suspect had fled. It led to a nearby vacant house where the front door was standing wide open. The dog was very focused on this house. Upon entering and searching the house they saw a trap door to the attic in a bedroom ceiling. There was a small amount of insulation on the floor, indicating perhaps someone had gone up there. Since officers were chasing a wanted felon who had shown he would not cooperate, I felt it too dangerous to have my officers poke their heads up into the attic. The K-9 officer knew his dog well and seemed to think there was a good chance our guy was up there. Other officers containing the area had meanwhile checked surrounding yards without success.

Knowing the SERT (Special Emergency Reaction Team) had the right equipment to safely check the attic, I contacted the SERT sergeant. We did not need the entire team to respond, just a smaller team. This would be called a "limited deployment." Sergeant Tom Ellis responded with a team of six SERT officers. They began a quick scouting of the area, planning to contain the house and use a periscope device to check the attic. All the while, several officers were keeping the surrounding area contained. No one would be going into or out of the containment area.

We were all surprised when we suddenly heard a perimeter officer shout "Police! Stop!" Followed by "Taser, Taser, Taser," which was the required announcement when the Taser "Stun Gun" was about to be deployed. From seemingly out of nowhere, the wanted subject had emerged from a fenced yard and ran right toward Officer Ty Blair. This time the Taser darts did not miss. It was a hot day and the subject was shirtless and sweaty, so they stuck nicely in the torso. He dropped to the ground instantly. In seconds, the suspect was handcuffed and in custody.

By now you must be thinking, "Okay, so where did the suspect come from?" As I said, officers had checked the obvious places, such as yards, sheds, and parked vehicles. There was one place they did not check. This was a house surrounded by a cyclone fence. Inside the fence was a large dog that barked a lot. The officers figured the bad guy would not risk jumping the fence with that dog there. Well, there was a small camper trailer in the rear of the yard that apparently was unlocked. It seems the suspect figured he would take his chances with the resident's dog in order to reach the potential safety of the camper. It was about 90 degrees in Portland that afternoon. In the closed-up camper, it must have been 120. After over an hour in there, the suspect probably thought the police had gone, and he had enough of baking in the "oven." When he exited and made a break for it, he saw that police were still there. He ran anyway and met Officer Blair's Taser. Of course, the lesson learned by the police was to always do a complete search and make no assumptions.

Chapter 31

Barricaded in an RV

P ortland, like any other large metropolitan city, has as part of its mix a population of "homeless" persons. Some are living on the streets simply because they want to be there. Others are mentally ill individuals who are not receiving the social services and follow up care that had been promised. Some are alcoholics or drug addicts. Others are out of work and sometimes not aware of available social services assistance. The homeless are there for a myriad of reasons. They become a police problem when their presence or actions bother other people enough to generate a call to police.

A recent phenomenon has been "homeless in an RV." Whether owned when the person fell on hard times, or acquired in some other manner, old "Recreational Vehicle" motorhomes began appearing at various locations within Northeast Precinct. They were generally in poor condition, not licensed, and not insured. How would a homeless person pay for a license or insurance? How would they pay for an RV campsite? So, the derelict RV ends up parked on the street somewhere, creating an eyesore. The once functional bathrooms in these vehicles no longer work, so another neighborhood problem is created, about which I need not elaborate.

One of these motorhomes was parked on a side street, in a residential area, only a short walk from the Portland Police Bureau's Northeast Precinct. The people who lived in the house adjacent to where the RV was parked felt sorry for the fellow who used it for his home. They were okay with it being there. Others in the neighborhood did not share that opinion. They wanted it gone. Over a period of weeks, parking patrol had hung numerous parking tickets on the RV. In Portland, it was illegal to park an unlicensed vehicle on a public street. The tickets remained unpaid, and a "tow warrant" had been issued. This would ultimately result in the vehicle being towed and impounded until all fines had been paid. Of course, towing charges and storage charges are incurred as well. If a parking patrol officer or a police officer calls for a tow, and the RV is unoccupied, it all goes routinely.

On this occasion, that was not to be the case. It was a warm summer day in Portland. Day shift in Northeast Precinct can be busy, but more so with routine calls than with tactical situations. A routine call came out to assist parking patrol with the removal of an old motorhome that had acquired a "tow warrant." Upon arrival of police, the homeless person, Wilbur Casey, happened to be inside when the officer knocked on the door.

The situation went rapidly downhill when the officer explained about the tow warrant and Wilbur refused to exit the motorhome. Routine calls can escalate in a heartbeat. The officer began to enter the motorhome when Wilbur backed into the recesses of the vehicle and picked up a simple steak knife. The officer deployed his Taser, a non-lethal electrical stun device, but the propelled probes missed Wilbur. Officer Clancy backed out and called for assistance from other officers and a supervisor.

My dayshift partner sergeant, Mike Schatler, responded. I dropped by in case additional supervisory assistance was needed. If this became a large tactical incident, multiple supervisors might be needed to handle various functions. We were conferring as to the next step, hesitant to call for the SERT (Special Emergency Response Team). The initial crime, menacing with a steak knife, was relatively insignificant. Calling the specialized team to extract Wilbur seemed to be overkill. However, an officer could not now just go in and grab him, nor could the police simply give up and leave.

As it happened, our Precinct Commander was returning from a meeting and dropped by. He agreed that we would not call SERT. Commander Bart Jones was level-headed, respected, and innovative. We talked about the situation and developed a plan.

Commander Jones correctly saw that a homeless person, and his or her RV, could be pushed around the City. These actions would in no way address the basic problems of the occupant. We had already pushed Wilbur all around Northeast Precinct. We contacted Wilbur Casey at a window of the RV, and convinced him to come to the Precinct and turn himself in. We promised that we would work on finding viable solutions for him. We also promised not to have his motorhome towed while we worked with him on a plan. He was skeptical and yet agreed to do as requested. We were committed to keeping our promises.

He showed up as planned and was cited for the menacing offense. We explained why this had to be done. We and a Neighborhood Response Team Officer then sat down with Wilbur and talked.

Wilbur told us he had been out of work for some time. He had been a mechanic, but his arthritis prevented him from doing that on a regular basis anymore. He said that he did not want to come out of the RV because it would be towed, and that he had no options as to housing or other shelter. As we continued to talk with Wilbur, we began to understand his plight. By the end of our meeting, Officer Mims of the Neighborhood Response Team agreed to help find solutions for Wilbur. We contacted the judge who signed the tow warrant, and, after the situation was explained, the judge agreed to cancel the warrant. We told Wilbur that no more citations would be issued while his situation was being addressed.

Officer Mims began making contacts. Community Mental Health assigned a caseworker. Since Wilbur was over sixty-five, the caseworker realized that he was eligible for Medicare and Social Security benefits. He saw a doctor and received needed medications. He had no idea that he was eligible for social security disability and other assistance. The Social Security Office was contacted, and arrangements were made for those benefits to be forthcoming. Social Services found a nice subsidized apartment for Wilbur. Volunteers helped Wilbur clean out the derelict RV and move any items which had value to his new home. Wilbur voluntarily relinquished the old RV to the scrapyard. The District Attorney's Office was contacted and the Menacing charge was dropped.

Follow-up contacts found that Wilbur Casey was now living a secure, normal life. As you might imagine, he became one of the Police Bureau's biggest supporters. For us at Northeast Precinct, he made a significant contribution. Too easily, we tend not to address the root problems of homelessness. It is more important to look for a permanent solution rather than just respond to the symptoms. Wilbur showed us that there is often a better way.

Chapter 32

Back in the Saddle Again

T he United States of America was engaged in a
war with North Korea in 1953. Seaman Daniel
Thompson, U.S. Navy, was assigned to the Shore
Patrol AWOL Apprehension Unit on the south side of
Chicago. The US Navy had a huge training facility just to
the north of Chicago, the Naval Station Great Lakes. In
fact, it was and is the U.S. Navy's only boot camp. Some
recruits occasionally tasted the night life in Chicago,
found a "girlfriend," and "forgot" to return to base. Then,
there were all the other AWOL sailors who went absent
for a variety of reasons. Seaman Thompson volunteered
to serve in this assignment. His Unit was headquartered
on the second floor of the Sixth District building of the
Chicago Police Department. In his assignment, Seaman
Thompson developed a close relationship with several
CPD officers. He knew what he wanted to do when he
completed his Navy service and was discharged the
following year.

It was a pleasant sunny spring morning in the City of Chicago. As nasty as Chicago winters are, spring is just the opposite. There are many spring days where there is just no other place you would want to be. Thirty-six recruits were to be sworn in as Chicago Police Officers at the Police Training Academy. Mr. Dan Thompson was to become Officer Dan Thompson. Most of the new hires had family present. Officer Thompson's wife proudly pinned his badge onto his uniform shirt. They had discussed this career move for countless hours, and she was fully supportive of his new endeavor. She fully realized the challenges that a police career can bring to a marriage.

Officer Thompson's training rotation included the usual stops at four different precincts and the traffic division. His talent for the job and the ability to interact with the public were noted in the required training evaluations. After the one-year probationary period, he served in assignments such as juvenile homicide and the plainclothes robbery detail.

The Chicago Police Department offered varied and exciting opportunities for an ambitious new police officer. However, there was one problem with being a cop anywhere in the 1950's. Six-day work weeks were the rule. There was no such thing as "overtime pay." Officers who were assigned a "late call," or were involved in a lengthy investigation, were expected to just suck it up and do the work. As one can imagine, this played havoc with an officer's home life. Rotating shift work and required court appearances also complicated the already topsy-turvy lives of police families.

For family reasons, Officer Dan Thompson made the decision to resign from the Chicago Police Department after eight years of service. He loved "the job" but left to pursue the challenge of new business opportunities that would provide a regular schedule and more time with his growing family. A potential higher level of income would also be good. With the full support of his family, he began a business venture. He was very successful with this, and the business income even provided enough money to give all his children the Catholic education that he and his wife felt was important. As the children reached their teenage years, the financial demands became less, and Dan began to think about again becoming a cop.

Opportunities began to arise in police departments of the small cities and suburbs south of Chicago. Over the years, compensation to police had improved quite a bit. It was time to get back in the saddle again. Dan sold his business and became Sergeant Dan Thompson, of the Beechwood Police Department. After two years, he had the opportunity to become Chief of Police in another small farming town in northeastern Illinois. He again enjoyed being a cop, but ethical dilemmas arose which, as he learned, were not too uncommon is small cities. It wasn't in the form of "payoffs" or anything like that, but more in terms of a "good old boys" network. Small town politicians seemed to think they were entitled to meddle in the work of their local police department. There came a point where Chief Thompson decided that he had quite enough of the meddling. He had maintained contact with a fellow with whom he had worked at the Beechwood PD. This individual had been hired by the Warren County, Iowa, Sheriff's Office, and told Chief Thompson about the opportunities in neighboring Jasper County. Dan & his wife talked it over and decided to make the move.

Deputy Dan Thompson settled right into his new role as a deputy sheriff of Jasper County, Iowa. Jasper County took in about 1,000 square miles east of the City of Des Moines. Once away from the Des Moines metropolitan area, the landscape changed to farms and small ranches, with some small towns here and there. The Sheriff's Office had established a sub-station near the town of Oakland Acres, to better serve the east area. Deputy Thompson was assigned to that sub-station.

It was not too long before Deputy Thompson's experience and abilities were recognized. The Sheriff promoted him to Sergeant, and then to Lieutenant, in charge of the Oakland Acres Substation. As a Lieutenant, he was quite concerned about the safety of the deputies in his command. They generally worked alone and help from other deputies could be a long way off. Aside from their handguns, the deputies all carried a twelve-gauge shotgun in their patrol cars.

Lieutenant Thompson was a firearms expert and knew, while the shotgun is a fine weapon for relatively close encounters, it was of little value should a deputy have to deal with a suspect, at a distance, armed with a rifle. And, there were plenty of rifles in the eastern part of Jasper County, owned by farmers, ranchers, and hunters. Additionally, there had been an increase in shootings involving street gangs in the Des Moines metropolitan area. Although the gang members were not known for being good shots, they did have some powerful weapons, usually taken in burglaries. He submitted a proposal that the deputies assigned to the Oakland Acres Substation be trained and armed with the Ruger 223/5.6 caliber semi-automatic rifle. This was a proven weapon, reliable and not difficult to shoot. The Sheriff approved the proposal. The deputies now had a tool which might one day save lives.

1994 was an election year. Elections included deciding who would be the Sheriff of Jasper County. Lieutenant Thompson supported the incumbent, for whom he worked. As it turned out, the opponent won. The Jasper County Sheriff's Office was like many such entities, in that appointments to rank were at the sole discretion of the sheriff. There was no merit system, nor any civil service protection. The new sheriff brought in a friend and appointed him as a Lieutenant to command the Oakland Acres Substation. Overnight, Lieutenant Thompson, who had done an exemplary job, became Deputy Thompson. Dan was not happy about it but took it well because, after all, that was how the system worked. He was still a cop and still enjoyed his job.

A couple years later, on March 13, 1996, Deputy Thompson was working day shift. Just coming on duty, it was too soon to stop for the usual coffee break at the Teapot Café. Shortly after 8:00 a.m., the drone of the police radio was broken by an emergency dispatch. Information was broadcast that a suspect had overpowered a Des Moines Police Department officer at a traffic stop. The location was US Highway 69 at Interstate 80. The suspect had handcuffed the officer to the officer's own patrol car and fled eastbound on I-80. The suspect's car was a Ford Fairlane with a powerful motor. Not known at the time, and thus not broadcast, was the fact that the suspect was armed with a Colt Model 1911 .45 caliber pistol. Later, it would be found that the suspect had taken this weapon in a burglary the day before at a Des Moines officer's home.

Deputy Thompson heard the broadcast and was close to I-80. He positioned his unmarked 1995 Chevrolet Caprice on the number 173 eastbound on-ramp to I-80, thinking that he might be able to intercept the suspect vehicle should it pass by. Chevrolet police cars of that era were fitted with Corvette motors and were well able to pursue practically anything on four wheels.

In mere moments, the suspect vehicle did come by on I-80 eastbound at a visibly high rate of speed. Deputy Thompson pulled out right on its tail, activating the emergency lights. The suspect was obviously not stopping, and Thompson obtained supervisory approval to pursue.

The suspect quickly exited the Interstate at the next opportunity, which was exit 179. The chase continued onto a combination of paved and gravel roads. Now, if you have ever flown over America's Heartland, you may recall glancing out the window of the airplane and seeing that the roads formed a checkerboard pattern, east-west, and north-south. The roads were needed to allow the farmers and ranchers to access their lands. Most of these were not paved because paving is expensive. However, they were generally well maintained with a gravel surface.

The suspect ended up turning onto East 150th Street South, a gravel road that went northbound from South 12th Avenue East. Speeds ranged from seventy-five to one hundred and five miles per hour. There was no other traffic, and fortunately a recent rain had prevented the suspect vehicle from generating huge dust clouds, so the deputy always had a clear vision of his quarry. It appeared to Deputy Thompson that the suspect did not know the area. It also seemed that he was attempting to return to Interstate 80.

As you can imagine, in the Heartland, construction costs do not allow the government to build underpasses/overpasses for every little gravel road that intersects the Interstate highway. Deputy Thompson knew this area well. The northbound road chosen by the suspect would terminate in a dead-end, about a mile south of I-80. There were no opportunities to turn east or west after the suspect executed the northbound turn. As the road ended, the suspect drove his vehicle into a muddy field and the vehicle became mired in the muck. An abandoned farmhouse was nearby, and the suspect ran into it. Meanwhile, two Iowa State Patrol officers had arrived to assist and ran to the house from the west to apprehend the suspect. Remember, at that point, no one knew that the suspect was armed. Deputy Thompson ran to cover the east side of the house, should the suspect exit the building.

As the State Patrol officers entered the abandoned farmhouse, the suspect emerged on the east side. Deputy Thompson was right there, only about seventy-five feet from the bad guy. He had grabbed his Ruger semi-automatic rifle as he jumped out of his patrol car. As soon as the suspect came into view, Deputy Thompson saw that the suspect had the Colt .45 pistol in hand. Thompson instantly worked the slide and chambered a round in the rifle. Twenty-nine additional rounds could be semi-automatically loaded as needed. Deputy Thompson saw an occupied house just to the east. He could not allow this fleeing armed felon to reach the house. If the suspect reached the house, it was highly likely that a hostage situation would develop. It looked as if Deputy Thompson would have to use his semi-automatic rifle to protect the lives of the occupants of the house. The suspect would likely die. This was the very type of rifle that had been fitted to the Oakland Acres Substation cars at his request, several years prior. He took aim and put his finger on the trigger, ready to fire.

The Iowa State Patrol officers were still searching the house, unaware that the suspect had run outside. There was no one else around. It would have been simple for the deputy to pull the trigger. However, Deputy Thompson took one last opportunity. The decision to use deadly force is the hardest decision a police officer will ever make. He ordered the suspect to put the gun down and lay down on the ground. The suspect hesitated but did not bring the Colt .45 up toward the deputy. If he had done that, his fate would have been sealed. But, the suspect did in fact lie down as ordered. Deputy Thompson commanded him to toss the gun away. The suspect complied. The Iowa State Patrol officers had, by now, emerged from the abandoned house, and handcuffed the suspect. Meanwhile, more Des Moines Police Department officers had converged upon the scene and the suspect was turned over to them.

The semi-automatic rifle fitted to the patrol car was there because Deputy Thompson, while a Lieutenant, had initiated a proposal establishing that the weapons were needed. As it turned out, without firing a round, he used this weapon to save a life. Whose life? When the suspect was taken back to Des Moines Police Headquarters, the suspect gave a statement. In this statement, the suspect said that he was ready to shoot it out with the police. However, he went on to say that, when he heard the round chambered into the rifle, and saw the deputy aiming it at him from seventy-five feet, he knew he would lose. Knowing that he would likely die, he wisely decided to give up. Certainly, Deputy Thompson had every justification to shoot the suspect. He did not shoot. It was close. Deputy Thompson was told by a Sheriff's Office supervisor that, had he shot the suspect, he likely would have received a Medal of Valor. Deputy Thompson was also told he would receive recognition at an awards banquet from both the sheriff's office and from Des Moines PD. He was ordered to appear in his "Class A" uniform. He and his family attended the banquet. Nothing was awarded. Nothing was even said. A bit stunned, after the ceremonies, they went home. It did not matter. Deputy Thompson knew he made the right decision. Just because an officer can use deadly force, does not mean that he should always do so. He continued to sleep well every night.

Chapter 33

The Black Cat

I was a night shift sergeant working in North Portland in 1991. Summer nights were usually enjoyable. We had low humidity, cooler temperatures, and lots of activity, especially on the weekends. The officers in my detail were a great group. I knew them well, and they were all capable and very cool-headed. That assignment continues to have been one of my favorites.

A "loud music" call came out at about 1:45 a.m. on a Tuesday night. This was not an unusual call. Many people had their windows open, and loud music does tend to disturb those with normal sleep patterns. Police go to the source of the noise, explain the situation, and most of the time people are cooperative and the problem is solved. Officer Johns was working beat 530 and caught the call.

Being a slow weeknight, myself and one other officer joined up with Officer Johns. You might say that we went along "for the ride." Unless the noise complaint call involved a big party or something that raised red flags, usually only one unit would be sent. This would generally be enough to deal with the problem. We parked our police cars a few doors down from the source of the music. You never, ever, pull up right in front of the subject address. Never. This is a standard police practice and is a safety procedure that is ingrained into all officers, no matter what the nature of the call.

If you are not a cop, I need to explain another point to you. Even on routine calls, as you approach the living unit, you gather intelligence. It is an automatic function and you do not even think about it. You use all your senses to accumulate knowledge. You never know what a "routine" call might turn into. So, if you can look in the windows and see who is inside, and what the layout is, it is all the better. You can start to assess the situation. You prepare. You look around for quick access to cover should shooting begin. Mostly, all is well. However, you never know. I have been involved in calls that went from "routine" to "life and death" situations in mere seconds.

We slowly crept up to the house through the darkness and peered through a huge picture window. We sized up the call. We saw the living area was brightly lit. Four guys who appeared to be Mexicans were sitting around the dining room table, cleanly dressed, playing cards. All looked quite normal, just some guys enjoying some camaraderie and having a fun game. We saw some beer cans on the table, but this was not unusual. We have all done the same thing. (Have you even been to a card party with a bunch of off-duty cops?) The Mexican guys had the volume on the radio quite high. Some lively Mexican tunes were being played. This looked like a very normal call which would be easy to resolve.

As we approached the front door, we saw a black cat on the walkway. We all had on our black leather gloves, which was normal attire for North Nights officers going on a call. Officer Rod Sorenson reached down and picked up Kitty. We all had the same thought and exchanged grins. The plan was all too obvious to us. Now, with his black gloves, Rod's grasp was invisible as he gently held Kitty around the mid-section.

Officer Johns knocked on a corner of the big picture window as Officer Sorenson held the cat in a standing position on the window ledge and moved Kitty in in such a way that Kitty appeared to be dancing to the music. The Mexican guys looked over and their eyes widened! They saw this cat dancing on the window ledge! Having had a few adult beverages, they thought it was really happening! They stared at each other in disbelief! It all must have looked like a funny television commercial.

After a few seconds, we showed ourselves. We saw that they began to smile and started laughing. All four came to the front door. We talked and we all had a good laugh. They understood and turned the music down. What a great way that was to resolve this call! I know we made some friends that night. We were not the expected officious cops. We were all real people and could all share a laugh together. A lot of times, a laugh and humor are not appropriate in police work. However, in this case it was the right course of action. We resolved the issue in a creative and fun manner. P.S. Kitty was sent on his way, not wanting to be a part of the discussion nor wanting to be a poker player.

Chapter 34

And the Chase Was On!

B eing a day shift sergeant at Northeast Precinct was a great job. Most of the officers on the shift had some degree of seniority. They had been around a bit, so a supervisor did not generally need to "rein them in," as with some of the younger, not-so experienced officers on other shifts. On day shift, officers and supervisors met many members of the public who seemed to appreciate that the police officer's job was not an easy one. They were usually reasonable and, while at times you may not have solved their problem entirely, you offered advice to guide them in a direction where help could be obtained. Officers did not have to routinely deal with the misfits that were commonly the focus of calls in the middle of the night. To keep life interesting on day shift, there were the occasional shootings, drug arrests, and other criminal activities which never seemed to take a complete rest.

Occasionally, vehicle pursuits do occur during day shift. Pursuits are very exciting entertainment for viewers of "Cops," or the typical Hollywood police drama programs. For police officers and sergeants, they are not entertaining at all. They are inherently dangerous and stressful. A myriad of considerations exist and vital decisions must be made during a "chase." Every police department has developed written general orders and procedures that must be followed in the event of a vehicle pursuit. Officers are expected to know and obey these rules. Sergeants are charged with the responsibility of monitoring and managing pursuits, ensuring that the rules are followed and that the risks inherent in a pursuit do not out-weigh the "reward" of catching the bad guy.

The "Risk/Reward" considerations can be illustrated by comparison to a teeter-totter. On one end, there is the crime and the criminal. On the other end, are the many risks involved, including injury to innocent members of the public, the pursuing officer, other officers, and to property. The more serious the crime and criminal, the more risk can be justified. A reasonable balance must be considered. If the risks begin to be greater than the reward of catching the criminal, the pursuit must be discontinued. As an example, suppose someone drives off with $100 worth of fuel from a gas station, without paying. An officer spots the suspect vehicle and gives chase. Soon the crook starts driving crazy, running red lights on a busy afternoon. There is a huge risk of an innocent person being seriously injured or killed, or of an officer suffering the same fate. All this for a hundred bucks worth of fuel? Not worth the risk! End of pursuit. Clearly the minor theft is not all that important in this scenario. Every pursuit in the City of Portland requires the sergeant managing the pursuit to write a detailed report following the incident, known as an "After Action Report." This report must include justification for all actions taken in the pursuit. The report is required no matter how short or long the event, or whether the pursuit was terminated in the interests of public safety. So, in summary, there is a huge responsibility involved with police pursuits. A lot of this responsibility falls on the shoulders of the sergeant.

It was a sunny and pleasant Tuesday afternoon in August, about 2:00 p.m. Summer weather in Portland is usually very nice. Not too hot and not at all humid, unlike weather in some other parts of the country. I had just stopped into a little bakery/coffee shop on NE 42nd Avenue, "Delphina's," for a coffee-to-go and a chocolate scone. I liked that bakery and often stopped there for morning coffee. The people working there were nice. The younger ones generally sported various tattoos and body piercings, but with age, I had learned to accept all that because really, it did not make any difference. I found that I developed good relationships with many of these folks. One of them even gave me some good leads on musicians that I would enjoy listening to. Also, I usually had some good interactions with some of the citizens who also would be there for their morning coffee. Another advantage of day shift: positive contacts with the community.

I had just gotten back into my police Crown Victoria Ford when I heard the call on the air of an armed robbery, with a shot fired, at the liquor store on Hayden Island. Hayden Island is located along the south side of the Columbia River, separating Oregon and Washington. It is an island because, on the south side of the island, there is a slough. The river and the slough come together and surround the island with water. Hayden Island incorporates a good-sized shopping center, and many stores in "strip malls" on the perimeter roads. The only vehicle access to "The Island" is via on/off ramps to the Interstate 5 Freeway. To a crook, it is kind of a "roll of the dice." There is quick and easy access to the freeway. In seconds, the bad guy can head north and be in Washington if he or she desires. Southbound, I-5 branches out after a few miles into different freeways. The downside to the crook is that the freeway is the only way to leave the island, other than via water by using a boat or taking a swim.

Call information came in of two bad guys who went into the liquor store. One displayed a handgun and shot a round into the ceiling just before he demanded money. The clerk acted quickly, ran, and locked herself in the secure back room, dialing 911. As it happened, a bystander, not seen by the bad guys, heard the shot and saw the two bad guys emerge and jump into a waiting car, motor running, with a third suspect at the wheel. This witness did the right thing, and immediately dialed 911 on his mobile phone. He was able to give a very accurate description of the getaway car, including the correct license plate number. This was broadcast immediately.

The crooks drove over to the nearby freeway and were probably trying to decide which entrance ramp to take. As luck would have it, the beat officer, Officer John Morley, had heard all the information and, in responding to the call, found that his path had converged with that of the suspect vehicle. He activated his lights and siren as he broadcast his location. The suspect vehicle was near a ramp that exited from northbound I-5 onto Hayden Island. In a panic, the "wheelman" went southbound (the wrong way) on this northbound ramp and entered I-5. This was mid-afternoon and there was a lot of traffic, creating a situation where the pursuit would need to be terminated quickly, even if the bad guys had to be let go for the moment. Fortunately, the driver made a tight U-turn, right on the freeway as other traffic skidded to a stop. The suspect vehicle headed northbound, now with traffic. By this time two other Portland Police Units had joined in behind Officer Morley. The pursuit then crossed the Columbia River Bridge and went into Vancouver, Washington.

As the sergeant supervising this incident, a lot went through my mind. First, Officer Morley was the primary pursuit vehicle. Officer Morley was an experienced officer, and a member of the SERT Team (Special Emergency Reaction Team), known in some other departments as "SWAT." He was level-headed, and if it came to a shooting, he would not miss. Secondly, pursuits into Washington State were strictly limited by Portland Police Bureau General Orders. Only crimes involving a serious forcible felony justified such a pursuit. In this pursuit, we had that covered. An armed robbery with a shot fired certainly fit the criterion. However, arrangements needed to be made to hand this pursuit over to police in Washington, specifically to the Vancouver, Washington, Police Department. Radio personnel were dealing with that task. We would continue the pursuit until the handoff to Washington authorities could be made. Using lights and siren, I made my way over to the I-5 area, about 10 minutes away. For a day shift sergeant to activate lights and siren, the incident had to be very "special."

Meanwhile, the three Portland Police Units were right on the bad guy's tail. Vancouver Washington PD was attempting to take over the pursuit, but momentarily had their hands full as the bad guy car went through a few red lights and nearly caused collisions. Fortunately, the Vancouver PD units were positioned to block traffic at intersections to protect the public. They did an excellent job. For some unknown reason, the suspect vehicle suddenly entered an on-ramp to I-5 southbound, heading back across the Columbia River to Portland. Vancouver PD never had chance to take over the pursuit. I suppose the Vancouver Police supervisors were quite happy about that. The bad guys were now back in our patch.

My three Portland Police Units were still right on the bad guys as they crossed the Columbia River Bridge. They sped southbound, weaving in and out, amidst medium daytime traffic on I-5, at 70-80 mph. Officer Matt Douglas, who was involved in the chase asked for "permission to ram." I knew Matt well and respected him. He was generally level-headed and very capable.

However, this was a situation where the supervisory "kibosh" was needed. A "ram" is uncontrolled contact with the other vehicle. In a "ram," you have no idea where either vehicle will end up, especially at high speeds. I could only visualize the bad guy's car jumping the I-5 center divider and crashing at high speed head-on into two or three innocent motorists who were northbound. I got on the air right away and said "No, but if you can do a PIT (Pursuit Intervention Technique), go ahead."

The PIT is used by many progressive police departments to bring an early end to vehicle pursuits. The quicker a pursuit can be concluded, the less risk there is to anyone involved, especially to the public. In departments that have adopted the PIT, the patrol cars are fitted with an arrangement of bars around the front end and leading edges of the front fenders of the patrol car. This protects the sheet metal. To execute a PIT, the officer chooses a "safe" area, preferably a wide street with some "run off" area to either side of the traffic lane. The officer begins to pull closely abreast of the suspect vehicle, on either side. When the officer's front wheel is adjacent to the suspect vehicle's rear fender area, the officer makes a quick quarter-turn of the steering wheel, toward the suspect vehicle. Planned contact with the suspect vehicle causes it to spin. If the PIT is done properly, little or no damage to the vehicles will occur. Hopefully, the suspect vehicle's motor will then stall. The officer who executes the PIT continues for a bit, and the two or three assisting patrol vehicles move into a position to take control of the suspect vehicle, as it spins to a stop and the motor quits. This is a safe and effective strategy. However, if speeds are over 40-50 mph, the technique can only be used in connection with serious crimes since the speeds involved do have greater consequences in terms of potential injuries and property damage per the laws of physics. We practiced this tactic over and over at our annual "In-Service Training." All officers mastered the PIT, and in fact many could hardly believe that training could be such "fun!"

Here is another strange "aside" about the PIT. For some time, Training Division had been trying to have this technique adopted as an approved strategy. A certain Deputy Chief of Police was in command of the Operations Division, which included Patrol. This person did not like any metal-to-metal contact, however slight, between police cars and suspect cars. The day after this person retired, Training Division presented this program to the new Deputy Chief of Operations. It was quickly approved. That is how things work in police departments.

Now let us return to the pursuit. The bad guys had been southbound on Interstate 5, with the three Portland Police cars right behind them. Fond of "wrong way maneuvers;" they just passed the I-5 southbound entrance ramp from Portland Boulevard when the driver did another quick U-turn on the freeway and proceeded to exit, northbound up the southbound on ramp. The Oregon Department of Transportation maintains cameras at selected locations and immediately notified police radio that the bad guys had abandoned the car at the top of the ramp on Portland Blvd and fled on foot. Several Portland Police units and I arrived. With the help of North Precinct Sergeant Reanna Lee, we set up a containment perimeter extending a few blocks in each direction. We were sure that we had the suspects contained somewhere within that area.

One nice feature of a big city is that there are a lot of cops to help in any emergency incident. The responding officers locked down the area. We had help from every precinct. The routine calls would have to wait. We had armed bad guys contained somewhere within the perimeter. We might end up with a hostage situation. We called our specialists, the SERT team. (Special Emergency Reaction Team) We designated a staging area for their deployment. This well-trained and armed team would execute a block by block, house by house search of the containment area, until we had our bad guys. It did not take long. They went "to ground" under a porch, not two-hundred feet from where they ditched the car. These SERT guys are very intimidating. When our bad guy threesome saw the team of SERT officers, with several AR-15 rifles pointed at them, it did not take but a split second for them to surrender.

No crashes. No injuries. The trio of armed robbery suspects were arrested with no shots fired. This was an excellent result. Of course, the mandatory "After-Action" report would need to be written by myself, justifying every decision that I made. This had been a very complex pursuit. Not a problem. I had it all mentally in order before getting back to the precinct. Once submitted, there was not one question asked of me regarding the actions taken. This was but another fun afternoon in the day of a sergeant.

Chapter 35

"The Z Man"

E very police sergeant, at every assignment, works with an officer whom he or she wishes they could clone. My officer was "The Z Man." I think that it was some time in the early 90's when I first met the "Z Man." Mark Zylawly, who became known as the "Z-man," had come to us from a little town somewhere in Montana. For quite some time, the Z Man had been on another shift. Even so, I had come to know his reputation.

Most police departments are quite gossipy. An officer's reputation is established quickly and tends to follow him or her along throughout their career. Let this be a caution to all young aspiring officers. Start off on the right foot, or you will spend years overcoming an early mistake.

When I came to Northeast Day Shift, as a sergeant, the "Z Man" was in my detail. This meant I was his assigned supervisor. Even though our days off and workdays were not quite in harmony, as his sergeant, I was the "go between," for any matters involving him and the brass in the downtown Portland "Ivory Tower." "Z Man" worked patrol district 640. He had Monday, Tuesday, and Wednesday off. So, he was scheduled to work Thursday, Friday, Saturday and Sunday. And work he did. His district was full of narcotic addicts and people who had a multitude of problems.

"Z Man" was smart and had a photographic memory. He knew who had active warrants. He would see them on the street and scoop them up. If they needed to be back in a treatment center, he made sure that happened. He was so sharp that, sometimes, he would spot another subject wanted on a warrant while he had one already in custody in the back seat of his patrol car. That created a problem.

You see, if you have a person in custody, handcuffed in the back of your patrol car, he or she is your responsibility. If any harm comes to them, it is in your pocket. "Z Man" knew his "clients" so well that, with the one subject in custody on the way to jail, he felt that he had to take another person he spotted into custody as well. "The Z Man" would stop and scoop up subject #2.

Now, supposing something unexpected takes place? Perhaps subject #2 pulls a gun and opens fire. A stray bullet hits the prisoner, handcuffed in the back seat of the police car. Or, the prisoner is a known gangster, and while "Z Man" is occupied, a rival gangster comes by and either shoots or kidnaps the prisoner? Sure, this is extreme, but it can happen. Sergeants must deal with the "what ifs?"

So, I had to have a talk with "Z Man" after roll call one morning. I told "Z" how much I valued him in my detail, and what a good job he did. I meant every word of it. But then I said, "Z, make no mistake, if you have one subject in custody, and stop for another, and something happens to your custody, you are in deep trouble. As well as everyone respects you and your work, the brass in the Ivory Tower downtown will hang you out to dry. They will not back you. There is nothing I would be able to say or do to help you." This got his attention. From then on, I think he understood.

Several months after this conversation, I retired. One Sunday morning in December, I got a phone call at home from a Northeast Precinct Supervisor. Bill knew that I would want to be informed as to what had occurred. The Z Man was dead.

"The Z Man" lived in Estacada, Oregon, about thirty miles east of Portland. He and his wife had two children and were a storybook family. It was a foggy Sunday morning in the winter. The hours of daylight were limited. "The Z Man" would have had to have left home at a pre-dawn hour, in order to reach the precinct in time to put on his uniform and be ready for the 7:00 a.m. roll call. He never made it.

For some reason, his older pickup truck had some mechanical issue, and he stopped on the shoulder of Interstate 84 westbound to investigate the cause of the problem. The hood was up. A fog blanketed the area and visibility was limited. There was little traffic. From what the Oregon State Police could determine, "The Z Man" must have been doing something under the hood and stepped into the roadway in order to get back in the truck and perhaps try to start it. He walked right into the path on an eighteen-wheeler semi-truck. Death was instantaneous.

All of us "blue suits" asked "why"? We had a hard time understanding how an experienced officer, knowing traffic hazards, could walk into a traffic lane on a freeway? A typical citizen—sure, but not a veteran cop! Maybe he was only half awake and focused on the truck's problem? We will never know.

My bride Marie & I went to the funeral. I told her in advance that police funerals are something very emotional and special. I had been to three, but this was her first. We sat for the testimonials and the stories. We learned that the black community had held a march to commemorate "The Z Man" and honor him for the job that he did in the community. What a tribute this was to a great officer and his work!

We, and most others present, shed tears. Many of you readers think we never do that. Well, if we come to a serious incident, we do not shed tears. We have work to do. That is what you want. You do not want us to sit down and cry with you. We may feel like it, but we do not. You want us to sort it out and catch the bad guy. On this occasion, our police family came together. We could shed tears. And we did. And as I write this chapter and rewrite it over and over, I still do.

Chapter 36

Why Your Cop Friends
Are Not Surprised

M any of you, not employed in law enforcement, have cop friends or relatives whom you meet at various social gatherings. Sometimes the conversation turns to some horrific event. You are a little perplexed, in that they react very calmly, or do not react at all, to what has been said. Police officers have seen so much in their line of work that nothing surprises them anymore. Perhaps they are amazed, but not at all surprised. Maybe this story will explain some of it.

Officer Len Smith was on patrol in the area that included N.E. Marine Drive and the Portland International Airport on a relatively quiet Wednesday evening. It was a misty, chilly fall night, as is common in Portland. There were a couple "pull-off" lots on Marine Drive, where people could pull off in their cars, park, and watch the aircraft take off and land. Of course, occasionally some of the "plane watchers" would get distracted and venture into more amorous activities that did not involve the observation of aircraft.

I will digress a bit. When I was growing up on the south side of Chicago, a lot of us hormonally driven teens hung out in the near south suburbs. One of the suburbs was called Riverdale. There was a Cook County park on the Cal-Sag Canal, and the channel at that point formed the eastern boundary dividing the City of Chicago and The Village of Riverdale. We called this park "TLP." This was our abbreviation for "Tail-Light Park." The unwritten rule with Riverdale law enforcement was, if a guy wanted to park there with his gal pal of the evening, and do some heavy "making-out," it was okay, as long as you had your parking lights on! If the parking lights were not on, then a Riverdale police officer was sure to come knocking on your window to ensure that all was well.

However, that was not quite the rule at the pull-off lots on Marine Drive. Officer Smith was conscientious in his patrol duties and, as time permitted, checked on each of the parked cars, which were generally occupied. Most were routine contacts. On this evening, however, Officer Smith was a bit amazed at what his eyes beheld. As Smith made his way through the lot, checking on the occupants of about ten vehicles parked off Marine Drive in the 7000 block, he knocked on one window while shining his high-powered flashlight into the interior. In a split second, he saw a lone male in the driver's seat, about 38 years of age. The male was turned around backwards in the seat and fondling the breasts of a totally naked female who was in the back seat. She appeared to be about thirty-eight years old. Officer Smith's gaze then shifted further into the backseat area, where he saw that she was also actively engaged in sexual intercourse with a young male, no more that fourteen years old, completely naked!

It was obvious to Office Len Smith that something very wrong was happening here. He called for two more cars, so that the occupants could be separated and questioned apart from one another. Meanwhile, the woman and the young boy were directed to put their clothes back on. The cover cars arrived in moments, and the two adults were handcuffed and placed in separate police vehicles. Officer Smith put the juvenile male in the back seat of his car, not handcuffed, as he appeared to be a victim and not a suspect.

A simple but bizarre story unfolded. The long and the short of it was that the two adults, being the male in the front seat and the naked female in the back seat with the young teen, were the teen's uncle and aunt! It seems that they had taken their nephew out for an evening of indoor go-karting. Leaving the facility, on the spur of the moment, they decided that it was time their nephew had his first sexual experience. Who would be better to teach him than a knowing and willing aunt? No one can guess why they thought it was a good idea to pull into the airplane-watching area to park their mobile classroom?

Officer Smith booked both adults into the county jail on serious felony charges, including Rape I. The young teenager was taken home. Officers, accompanied by a victim's advocate from social services (who said this was the first time she had assisted in this type of situation), ensured that the home situation was safe, and that appropriate follow-up counselling would be scheduled.

I am sure that most of you are thinking "this is sick." Yes, it is sick. Cops run into the sick and bizarre more often than you think. We just do not talk about it much. It is not that we do not feel; it is just that aberrant human behavior no longer surprises us. It comes with our jobs. That is why, in a non-police social setting, discussions come up about some very weird events, and we remain calm and quiet. We probably have stories that would easily top yours, but we just would rather not add them to the conversation.

Chapter 37

"731 to Dispatch: I'm Pursuing an Alien."

B y now, the reader has realized that the world of policing results in many varied scenarios. Many are hard to believe. A central theme is that many crooks, amateur and professional, think they are slick and will not be caught. This chapter will not be long. It is so funny that I needed to fit it in somewhere. It is so comical that I could not make it up. To appreciate it, you must mentally put yourself in the situation.

One fall evening, I was one of the sergeants on duty on the east side of Portland. It was a typical routine night. Funny, most nights start out that way. Of course, some shifts often end a bit differently. Dispatch gave out information on a burglary that "just occurred," in the suburb of Milwaukee, adjoining the City of Portland on the southern boundary.

A store that dealt in "collector" comic books, trading cards, etc., had just been burglarized. Thieves had smashed a display window and taken an eight-foot high statue of "Predator."

The giant "Predator" was displayed in the window to add a bit of spice to the store. For the uninitiated, "Predator" is an alien character in a 1987 movie, regarded as a classic in the genre. The movie is centered about a team of commandos, including a character played by the well-known Arnold Schwarzenegger. Their mission is ostensibly to rescue the victims of a helicopter crash deep in the jungles of Central America. Apparently, they were sent there on some type of pretext. They have no idea they would be hunted, for sporting purposes, by an extraterrestrial warrior known as "Predator," who came from another planet to enjoy the "thrill of the hunt." To appreciate the humor to follow, you really should take a few minutes to do an internet search and see what the character "Predator" is all about. You would hardly want to meet him in a dark alley. He is very scary.

The trouble is that many crooks, especially young ones, usually do not plan very far ahead. Often, they act impulsively, with little thought as to how to complete their scheme. Consequently, these young miscreants had no viable plan for making their escape with "Predator." They did not mentally get past the thought of "Hey, I've got a good idea!"

Thus, once liberated from the confines of the second-hand store front display window, the alien "Predator" needed to be spirited off. The burglars escape car of choice (or maybe just of circumstances) was a mid-seventies Plymouth Valiant. These cars had a good-sized trunk, but hardly large enough to house the alien "Predator." After all, he was about eight feet tall! Thus, they stuffed him in as best they could, with about four feet of "Predator" flopping around outside the partially closed trunk lid. You can imagine what this looked like as the escape vehicle fled the scene of the crime. Milwaukee Police Department units were quick to spot the suspect vehicle. They activated lights and sirens, but the vehicle did not stop and thus the pursuit began. In moments, the vehicle crossed over the municipal border into the City of Portland.

This was not a difficult vehicle to spot, as the Milwaukee Police Department vehicles, and the fleeing Plymouth Valiant, came over the Ross Island Bridge. Pursuits originating in other jurisdictions are handed off to the appropriate jurisdiction when they enter the new area. As the fleeing Plymouth continued into East Portland from Milwaukee and crossed the Ross Island Bridge, Portland Unit 731 took up the pursuit.

Once again, I will state that vehicle pursuits are very serious. There are a myriad of decisions officers and supervisors must make on the spur of the moment, and the decisions had better be right. Yet, upon occasion, there is a lighter side to even the most serious of police matters.

The chase wound into the Portland's west hills. There was not time to hand it off to Central Precinct Units, who had responsibility for the west hills. The Southeast Portland Police Precinct unit thus continued the chase. Two or three other Southeast Precinct Portland units had meanwhile joined in. Having served in both police precincts, I can tell you that, unless you are assigned to a south-west hills beat for a goodly period, you have no idea where the roads are going. There are all sorts of twists and turns, and dead-end roads where "you can't get there from here," regardless of what the map said. The burglars were no more knowledgeable of the terrain than were the southeast officers. It did not take too long for the burglars to lose control of their vehicle, sending it crashing into a dirt bank and stalling. These aspiring burglars did not have much skill in evasive driving tactics. Portland Police officers were right on their tail, taking the three suspects into custody in short order.

But, what about the kidnapped alien "Predator," who had been helplessly stashed in the trunk of the Plymouth, his lower extremities flopping about? He was quickly removed from the trunk of the disabled Plymouth Valiant, and was standing tall and basking in the floodlights, provided by courtesy of the responding Portland Fire Bureau units. "Predator" may as well have been on the set of a Hollywood movie, ready to spout his lines. He seemed no worse for wear after all the flopping about during the chase. As a supervisor, I had been headed that way and was prepared to gather the required information needed to complete my obligatory report, not quite ready for the scene which was about to unfold.

As I arrived several minutes after the chase ended, and exited my police car, I broke into uncontrollable laughter. My officers had surrounded the posed alien "Predator," snapping endless "Polaroid" photos of themselves and "Predator." It was a funny sight to see, and the officers were certainly enjoying themselves. (For those who do not know what a "Polaroid Camera" is, it was a brand of camera that took photos and developed them internally within a minute, and then spat them out to the waiting photographer. These enjoyed some popularity in the "pre-digital" days.) General Orders mandated that all officers be equipped with these cameras, and they were put to good use, aside from their stated purposes, on this occasion. I know that these photos were never entered into evidence, and I did not ask about them any further. We all had quite a good laugh over this most unusual pursuit. It was all good fun in the end! As to Predator, the shop owner responded and took him back to his place of safety. The youthful burglars went to jail.

As I submitted my "After Action" report, I laughed to myself as I thought that "The Brass" downtown would take it as some type of a joke. Yet, it was all true. Sometimes police work results in some unbelievable, yet very comical situations.

Chapter 38

The Hardest Decision a Cop Will Ever Make

Since you are reading this book, I assume you are interested in police work. I wrote this book to provide a glimpse of the many varied situations police encounter. This book was not written primarily for cops, but, if you are or have been in law enforcement, I thank you for reading it, and hope that you too have enjoyed the stories.

The topic of deadly force really needs to be discussed, but I could not find a practical way to weave it into a story. For this chapter, I will depart from the police story format. I think it is an important enough topic to include in this book.

From time to time, the topic of police involved shootings arises in my conversations with friends and acquaintances. I have had discussions with people from the USA, Canada, England, and Australia. Quite often, people ask "Why don't the police just shoot the person in the arm or leg, and avoid killing him or her?" A lengthy discussion follows, and I think I have been successful in explaining the reasons why police cannot and do not attempt to do that.

Let us be very clear that no law enforcement officer starts his or her shift with the thought "Gee, maybe I'll have a chance to shoot someone today." Cops do not want to have to use deadly force and yet recognize that at some time they may have no choice but to do so. The use of deadly force is generally authorized when officers reasonably believe that it is necessary to protect themselves or others from death or serious bodily harm.

There is a wealth of information available on the internet regarding police involved shootings. Policeone. com is one source. On that site, a retired sergeant, expert in firearms and firearms training, said: "Officer involved shootings are generally dynamic and short lived. They occur at close distances and often take place in diminished lighting conditions." In the process of planning presentations for seminars and publications, Calibre Press, publisher of Street Survival II, examined extensive research regarding officers killed with firearms. The research shows that, in recent years, about fifty-one percent of the officers killed were shot between zero and five feet and an additional twenty percent were shot from six to ten feet. Thus, over seventy percent of the officers killed by firearms were in close contact situations! Further research in the studies examined by Calibre Press shows that a suspect can raise and fire a weapon in .39-.59 of a second. The average officer takes 1.9 seconds to draw, raise, and fire his or her weapon, without aiming. Bearing this in mind, is it any wonder officers seem a bit "on guard" when contacting citizens? Clearly, the more distance there is between the officer and a suspect, the safer it is for the officer.

At any call, the officer must rely upon training, knowledge of the law, and a split-second assessment of the circumstances at hand. There is no time to sit and ponder all these decision factors. A routine call or contact can turn into a deadly force situation just as quickly as you can snap your fingers. Every officer deserves to go home safely at the end of his or her shift. There must be no hesitation when an officer must act. However, the decision must be correct.

Police involved shootings cannot be likened to shooting stationary duck cut-outs at a carnival. The person threatening the officer's life is not standing still, just waiting for the officer to aim and shoot. No. The suspect is generally moving; arms and legs are in motion, sometimes the person is charging at the officer. Think about how hard it would be to hit an arm that was flailing about. The only part of the suspect that the officer has a reasonable likelihood of striking is the torso. There is no time to take careful aim. It often is essentially a "point and shoot" situation.

In timed police firearms training, police use targets of a human silhouette. Different parts of the body outline have different point values. The chest/torso area has a value of five, in that vital organs are contained in that area. Other areas have lesser values. Bullets striking the "Five-X" area are most likely to incapacitate the target. Police do not "shoot to kill," but of course sometimes the shots are fatal. The idea is to stop the threat from doing whatever action he or she was taking that necessitated the use of deadly force in the first place.

Once the decision is made to shoot, the officer will continue to shoot only until the threat is neutralized. This is generally when the suspect drops to the ground. As long at the threat keeps advancing or moving, the officer cannot tell if the shots were effective in stopping the threat or if the shots even hit the threat. Sometimes one or two shots have accomplished that goal. Sometimes it takes many more. Perhaps some of the shots missed? Maybe the bad guy was wearing body armor? Yes, they occasionally do. There have been instances where a subject has taken several hits to the torso area, and yet remained standing! Officers should not be criticized for firing multiple shots. Each situation is unique.

Once the suspect is down, the officer or officers will cautiously approach if possible. They must be on the alert for any indication that the suspect is still armed with a deadly weapon, and feigning incapacity. The suspect will be handcuffed quickly to ensure officer safety. Then, emergency medical services (EMS) personnel, will have been summoned, or called in from their "standby" positions, to attend to the suspect. Even if the suspect appears to be deceased, this is still required. Officers are not qualified to pronounce the status of the subject who was shot. Remember, the goal was not to "kill" the suspect. The goal was to stop the suspect from engaging in behavior that threatened lives. If the suspect is still alive and can be helped by EMS, that is just fine.

Another question that I often answer is: "Well, why not fire a warning shot. That would get their attention." Most law enforcement agencies prohibit the use of "warning shots." There are two primary reasons for this prohibition.

First, there is no telling where that "warning shot" will end up. Bullets travel long distances. I recall an incident in one city where a couple gangsters shot at one other in the downtown area. One stray bullet went about a half a mile and hit an innocent man in the head, killing him. Additionally, many incidents occur in an urban environment. Bullets can bounce off many types of surfaces, especially concrete.

Secondly, and perhaps of more importance, is the phenomenon known as "sympathetic fire." Let us say that a situation has arisen where the officer might have to use deadly force but not yet be justified in doing so. The officer fires a "warning shot." Other officers have meanwhile arrived to assist. They hear the shot, and do not know whether it came from the officer's weapon, or the suspect's weapon. They do not know that it is a "warning shot." Remember, this is a fast-paced scenario. Perhaps there was no time to put this information out on the radio. Either way, they figure that there is a reason to shoot. The situation has not actually escalated to a point where the officer who fired the "warning shot" can justify shooting the suspect. Yet, the suspect is struck as a result of sympathetic fire by assisting officers. Not a good situation. And really, a "warning shot" would do nothing to heighten the suspect's attention.

Another question that sometimes arises is: "Well, don't officers have Tasers, batons, and pepper spray? Why not use those instead of shooting?" These are what law enforcement calls "non-lethal force." Tasers, batons, and pepper spray, absent any rare circumstances, are not likely to cause death or serious injury. They are tools used to subdue combative subjects who are threatening others, or even themselves (suicidal persons). At the point where one of these tools is considered, the subject's behavior is not threatening anyone with death or serious physical injury. Should an officer prepare to use a Taser or pepper spray, or even a baton, his or her hands are tied up with that tool. If a deadly force situation suddenly develops, he or she would need to get rid of that item in order to draw his or her firearm. Seconds are critical.

There are times when these tools may be used in a situation that officers know might escalate into a deadly force incident. A tactic known as "lethal cover" is used. One officer might be taking aim at the subject, ready to use his or her firearm, if need be. A second officer meanwhile deploys the Taser. Officers use sound tactical procedures, yet take an extra step, if possible, to avoid shooting. This is a common scenario in dealing with some suicidal subjects. Note that batons and pepper spray are not used in these cases, because the officer would generally need to be too close to the subject for safety.

In covering an officer-involved shooting story, the media often note that the officer "has been placed on administrative leave." What does this really mean? Following a shooting, whether the suspect lives or dies, the officer is relieved of duty and stays home, or at least remains available. Meanwhile, the incident is reviewed. Detectives investigate the use of deadly force, just like a criminal case. Often the agency's own detectives handle this. There is not a problem with this if the agency has a lot of experience in these matters. Even if the investigators were tempted to skew the facts, they cannot and would not do so. They know full well that the incident will be thoroughly reviewed by attorneys who are expert in finding any flaws. Simultaneously, police administrators review the incident to ensure that the officer complied with all general orders and procedures. At the same time, the District Attorney's Office reviews the case in order to present the facts to a Grand Jury. The Grand Jury, composed of ordinary citizens, will determine if a crime has or has not been committed. If the use of deadly force was not justified, the officer will likely face criminal prosecution. As you can see, officers are fully accountable for the action that they have taken.

As noted in the above paragraph, the officer will be interviewed by detectives. It may surprise you, but the officer must be advised of his or her right to an attorney. The courts have ruled that persons need to know that their statements can and will be used against them in court. I will not digress into a lengthy explanation, but if person, even an officer, has requested an attorney and been denied access to one, any statements the person makes will not be admissible in court. Most departments, in the past, have allowed some time to pass before interviewing an officer who used deadly force. There is a significant body of research that has found that, following a deadly force incident, memory is, for a time, clouded and sometimes not accurate. Thus, the passage of several days before the interview will generally result in the officer relating a clearer and more accurate story of the events that transpired. With his or her lawyer present, the officer will be ordered to respond to the questions that are posed. This process ensures a solid investigation, while protecting the officer's constitutional rights.

A disturbing trend has developed. Some departments are having detectives interview the officer as soon as possible after the use of deadly force. Furthermore, these departments are denying the officer the right to consult with and have an attorney present during questioning. This is not a sound procedure, and if the use of deadly force was not justified, none of the officer's statements can be used in a criminal prosecution. In this writer's opinion, this is a step backward.

In any event, "administrative leave" is no holiday for the officer. Now, if the officer shoots a bank robber who was exiting the bank brandishing a weapon, he or she may be somewhat confident that the review, at all levels, will go well. However, supposing there was a shooting where, for example, the suspect was lawfully stopped and was combative, refused all orders, and was reaching in his waistband and quickly drew a shiny object. It was night-time. Visibility was poor. The officer, fearing that the shiny object was a small pistol, shoots the suspect. From the officer's perspective, this was reasonable. The shiny object turned out later to be a cell phone. Why would someone stopped for a traffic violation, or for another reason, want to argue with a well-trained officer whom he knows has a firearm? Many of these suspects just are not rational people. In another case, the weapon pointed at officers by the suspect turned out to be a pellet gun. Many pellet guns look exactly like the real thing. How was the officer to know this? Remember, these decisions are made in split seconds. The officer will spend weeks "on administrative leave," hoping that he or she is cleared of any wrongdoing. This is absolute hell for the officer.

A reality today is that nearly everyone has a phone with video capabilities. People can come across a police action and begin recording. Sometimes the news media airs these videos, or parts of them, putting officers in a bad light. There was a situation in California recently where the amateur video showed one perspective. Another video from a nearby business was located. The perspective from this video was different and justified all police actions taken. A video is only one part of the story. There are many other relevant factors, including the behavior of the subject prior to the recording, the possible influence of alcohol or drugs on the subject, oral communication between officers and subject, the overall physical setting, and observed or perceived weapons available to the subject. These and other factors provide a complete picture of the incident. Unfortunately, it seems that officers are often "tried by the media" well before all the facts are known. Anyone in the news media will tell you, privately, "If it bleeds, it leads." The audience ratings are important in the competitive news industry. This is often what drives coverage, even if a video does not present a complete picture of the event.

In conclusion, no officer wants to be in a deadly force situation and shoot another human being. No matter how well justified the shooting was when reviewed, it is a life-changing event for that officer. The officer had no other reasonable choice. Keep this in mind as you listen to the mass media coverage concerning officer involved shootings.

Chapter 39

The End?

Although this book has an ending, police work, wherever it is done, will never have an end. The types of incidents that have been detailed in this book occur every day, in every jurisdiction. Any experienced cop could write a similar book. All that needs to be done is to put it down on paper.

What I have tried to do is to bring the real world of policing into your hearts and minds. As stated in the Forward, it is not the "shoot 'em up" stuff that "Hollywood" has promoted. It is a world of panic, compassion, amazement, fun, service, and, occasionally, tears. It has been an experience that I would not trade, but, in today's climate, I do not think that I would entertain again. There is too much political and media attention given to decisions cops must make on the spur of a moment. To hesitate means that the officer could die. Many cops today are becoming a little reluctant to act, because they do not want to be "that guy" on a video.

Thus, routine stops, field interrogations etc., occur less often. The crooks are indeed getting the "upper hand."

A police career presents all types of "landmines." There can be stress, abuse of alcohol, maybe even drug abuse, demands of shift work, marital strife and divorces (sometimes multiple) with which to deal. If you pursue a police career, I wish you well. I hope you have as much fun as I did, and that you can survive it. Consider carefully exactly what you are getting into. A good friend of mine, a retired State Trooper, told me of the wife of a newly hired Trooper, who telephoned the Superintendent of State Police, wondering why on earth her husband couldn't have Christmas day off so he could be with be with the family! I do not know what the outcome was, but I expect their marriage did not last much longer. She just did not get it. Not only the officer, but his or her family, is called upon to make sacrifices.

Police work is hard and usually thankless. Show your support for the officers. Maybe smile and wave (with all fingers please). I have been eating supper at one of my favorite "police-friendly" restaurants and found that another patron who had already left had, unbeknownst to me, paid for my meal. What a great gesture of thanks that was! Of course, I could not accept a gratuity, but it was too late. Think about doing something similar if the opportunity presents itself. In any way possible, please show appreciation to the cops. They are doing a job that most people could not or would not do. They are protecting you, 24/7, and occasionally make the greatest of all sacrifices. They give their lives.

Appendix

For Further Reading

The author suggests the following books, for those who enjoy reading about real crimes, investigations, and prosecutions. He has received no compensation or other consideration for these recommendations.

Alcatraz from the Inside, by Jim Quillan. Life "On the Rock" as told by a former inmate, with a good ending. I have visited Alcatraz. Do not miss the opportunity if you are in San Francisco.

I Heard You Paint Houses, by Charles Brandt. This is a true account of a man's life in "The Mob," with revelations about Jimmy Hoffa's "disappearance" and the assassination of John F. Kennedy.

Ripper, by Linda Rosencrance. The story of the victims and a serial killer in Rhode Island is told in chilling detail.

The Crime of the Century: Richard Speck & the Murders that Shocked the Nation, by Dennis Breo. The story of eight student nurses and their killer that took place on the South Side of Chicago did indeed shock the nation. Solid detective work by Chicago Police resulted in a speedy arrest. The author of **Cop Talk** grew up in his teens not far from the area where the crime took place and recalls it very well.

Murder in Spokane: Catching a Serial Killer, by Mark Fuhrman. A veteran detective reviews and analyzes the murders, showing how authorities placed too much reliance upon computers and technology. Good basic police work could have caught Richard Yates two years earlier and saved lives.

Any of Ann Rule's "true crime" books are well worth reading. All are well researched and documented in detail. There are too many books to list here.

The author generally prefers books about true incidents. However, there are two authors who have written fictional stories that are realistic with very plausible details:

Joe Wambaugh, who served fourteen years with the Los Angeles Police Department, is a master at creating police novels.

Sue Grafton has written an "alphabetical" mystery series, A through Y, featuring private investigator Kinsey Milhone. Even sound investigative procedures often result in Kinsey placing her life in danger. Ms.

Grafton's final book was to be "Z is for Zero." Sadly, she succumbed to cancer before she could write her last book and finish the series. Her series was written from 1982-2017.

Lastly, this writer strongly recommends a professional resource for police officers of any rank and jurisdiction. **Street Survival II: Tactics for Deadly Force Encounters**, by Lt. Dan Marcou & Lt. Jim Glennon, is published by Calibre Press. Officers should have this book as their Bible to be read and studied over and over. All content is relevant. This book is the best life insurance policy an officer could have. If you are a cop, buy it. If you are a friend or loved one of a cop, buy it for them.

CPSIA information can be obtained
at www.ICGtesting.com
Printed in the USA
LVHW031429231220
674968LV00006B/231